LES MISÉRABLES

Victor Hugo

EDITORIAL DIRECTOR Laurie Barnett
DIRECTOR OF TECHNOLOGY Tammy Hepps

SERIES EDITOR John Crowther
MANAGING EDITOR Vincent Janoski

WRITERS Brian Phillips, Deborah Forbes
EDITORS Thomas Connors, Matt Blanchard

This edition published by Spark Publishing

Spark Publishing
A Division of SparkNotes LLC
120 Fifth Avenue, 8th Floor
New York, NY 10011

Please submit all comments and questions or report errors to www.sparknotes.com/errors

Printed and bound in the United States

ISBN 1-58663-386-4

INTRODUCTION: STOPPING TO BUY SPARKNOTES ON A SNOWY EVENING

Whose words these are you *think* you know.
Your paper's due tomorrow, though;
We're glad to see you stopping here
To get some help before you go.

Lost your course? You'll find it here.
Face tests and essays without fear.
Between the words, good grades at stake:
Get great results throughout the year.

Once school bells caused your heart to quake
As teachers circled each mistake.
Use SparkNotes and no longer weep,
Ace every single test you take.

Yes, books are lovely, dark, and deep,
But only what you grasp you keep,
With hours to go before you sleep,
With hours to go before you sleep.

Contents

NOTE: This SparkNote refers to the Signet Classic edition of *Les Misérables*. Some abridged editions divide the novel into three volumes. In these editions, Volume One corresponds to "Fantine"; Volume Two to "Cosette"; and Volume Three to "Marius," "Saint-Denis," and "Jean Valjean."

CONTEXT

VICTOR HUGO was born in 1802 in the French town of Besançon. His father was a general in Napoléon's army, and much of his childhood was therefore spent amid the backdrop of Napoléon's campaigns in Spain and in Italy. At the age of eleven, Hugo returned to live with his mother in Paris, where he became infatuated with books and literature. By the time he was fifteen, he had already submitted one poem to a contest sponsored by the prestigious French Academy.

Hugo wrote prolifically in all genres, but his plays proved to be his earliest critical and commercial successes. France's 1830 July Revolution opened Hugo's creative floodgates, and he began producing a steady stream of work, most notably the novel *The Hunchback of Notre-Dame* (1831). Hugo also began to cultivate his interest in politics and was elected to France's National Assembly after the revolution of 1848. As Hugo grew older, his politics became increasingly leftist, and he was forced to flee France in 1851 because of his opposition to the monarch Louis Napoléon. Hugo remained in exile until 1870, when he returned to his home country as a national hero. He continued to write until his death in 1885. He was buried with every conceivable honor in one of the grandest funerals in modern French history.

Hugo remains one of the most popular and respected authors in French literature. His writings were cultural fixtures throughout the nineteenth century, and he quickly emerged as one of the leaders of the Romantic movement in literature. Hugo also developed his own brand of imaginative realism, a literary style that combines realistic elements with exaggerated symbolism. In this style, each character represents a significant social issue of the time. Indeed, political concerns dominate much of Hugo's writing, and he used his work to champion causes such as universal suffrage and free education. Hugo believed that the modern writer had a mission to defend the less fortunate members of society. Though he often drew criticism for his politics, his passion for documenting injustice ultimately led to widespread praise for both his literary and social achievements.

Hugo began writing *Les Misérables* twenty years before its eventual publication in 1862. His goals in writing the novel were as lofty as the reputation it has subsequently acquired; *Les Misérables* is primarily a great humanitarian work that encourages compassion and hope in the face of adversity and injustice. It is also, however, a historical novel of great scope and analysis, and it provides a detailed vision of nineteenth-century French politics and society. By coupling his story of redemption with a meticulous documentation of the injustices of France's recent past, Hugo hoped *Les Misérables* would encourage a more progressive and democratic future. Driven by his commitment to reform and progress, Hugo wrote *Les Misérables* with nothing less than a literary and political revolution in mind.

Les Misérables employs Hugo's style of imaginative realism and is set in an artificially created human hell that emphasizes the three major predicaments of the nineteenth century. Each of the three major characters in the novel symbolizes one of these predicaments: Jean Valjean represents the degradation of man in the proletariat, Fantine represents the subjection of women through hunger, and Cosette represents the atrophy of the child by darkness. In part, the novel's fame has endured because Hugo successfully created characters that serve as symbols of larger problems without being flat devices.

Plot Overview

THE CONVICT JEAN VALJEAN is released from a French prison after serving nineteen years for stealing a loaf of bread and for subsequent attempts to escape from prison. When Valjean arrives at the town of Digne, no one is willing to give him shelter because he is an ex-convict. Desperate, Valjean knocks on the door of M. Myriel, the kindly bishop of Digne. Myriel treats Valjean with kindness, but Valjean repays the bishop by stealing his silverware. When the police arrest Valjean, Myriel covers for him, claiming that the silverware was a gift. The authorities release Valjean and Myriel makes him promise to become an honest man. Eager to fulfill his promise, Valjean masks his identity and enters the town of Montreuil-sur-mer. Under the assumed name of Madeleine, Valjean invents an ingenious manufacturing process that brings the town prosperity. He eventually becomes the town's mayor.

Fantine, a young woman from Montreuil, lives in Paris. She falls in love with Tholomyès, a wealthy student who gets her pregnant and then abandons her. Fantine returns to her home village with her daughter, Cosette. On the way to Montreuil, however, Fantine realizes that she will never be able to find work if the townspeople know that she has an illegitimate child. In the town of Montfermeil, she meets the Thénardiers, a family that runs the local inn. The Thénardiers agree to look after Cosette as long as Fantine sends them a monthly allowance.

In Montreuil, Fantine finds work in Madeleine's factory. Fantine's coworkers find out about Cosette, however, and Fantine is fired. The Thénardiers demand more money to support Cosette, and Fantine resorts to prostitution to make ends meet. One night, Javert, Montreuil's police chief, arrests Fantine. She is to be sent to prison, but Madeleine intervenes. Fantine has fallen ill, and when she longs to see Cosette, Madeleine promises to send for her. First, however, he must contend with Javert, who has discovered Madeleine's criminal past. Javert tells Madeleine that a man has been accused of being Jean Valjean, and Madeleine confesses his true identity. Javert shows up to arrest Valjean while Valjean is at Fantine's bedside, and Fantine dies from the shock.

After a few years, Valjean escapes from prison and heads to Montfermeil, where he is able to buy Cosette from the Thénardiers. The Thénardiers turn out to be a family of scoundrels who abuse Cosette while spoiling their own two daughters, Eponine and Azelma. Valjean and Cosette move to a run-down part of Paris. Javert discovers their hideout, however, and they are forced to flee. They find refuge in a convent, where Cosette attends school and Valjean works as a gardener.

Marius Pontmercy is a young man who lives with his wealthy grandfather, M. Gillenormand. Because of political differences within the family, Marius has never met his father, Georges Pontmercy. After his father dies, however, Marius learns more about him and comes to admire his father's democratic politics. Angry with his grandfather, Marius moves out of Gillenormand's house and lives as a poor young law student. While in law school, Marius associates with a group of radical students, the Friends of the ABC, who are led by the charismatic Enjolras. One day, Marius sees Cosette at a public park. It is love at first sight, but the protective Valjean does his utmost to prevent Cosette and Marius from ever meeting. Their paths cross once again, however, when Valjean makes a charitable visit to Marius's poor neighbors, the Jondrettes. The Jondrettes are in fact the Thénardiers, who have lost their inn and moved to Paris under an assumed name. After Valjean leaves, Thénardier announces a plan to rob Valjean when he returns. Alarmed, Marius alerts the local police inspector, who turns out to be Javert. The ambush is foiled and the Thénardiers are arrested, but Valjean escapes before Javert can identify him.

Thénardier's daughter Eponine, who is in love with Marius, helps Marius discover Cosette's whereabouts. Marius is finally able to make contact with Cosette, and the two declare their love for each other. Valjean, however, soon shatters their happiness. Worried that he will lose Cosette and unnerved by political unrest in the city, Valjean announces that he and Cosette are moving to England. In desperation, Marius runs to his grandfather, M. Gillenormand, to ask for M. Gillenormand's permission to marry Cosette. Their meeting ends in a bitter argument. When Marius returns to Cosette, she and Valjean have disappeared. Heartbroken, Marius decides to join his radical student friends, who have started a political uprising. Armed with two pistols, Marius heads for the barricades.

The uprising seems doomed, but Marius and his fellow students nonetheless stand their ground and vow to fight for freedom and democracy. The students discover Javert among their ranks, and, realizing that he is a spy, Enjolras ties him up. As the army launches its first attack against the students, Eponine throws herself in front of a rifle to save Marius's life. As Eponine dies in Marius's arms, she hands him a letter from Cosette. Marius quickly scribbles a reply and orders a boy, Gavroche, to deliver it to Cosette.

Valjean manages to intercept the note and sets out to save the life of the man his daughter loves. Valjean arrives at the barricade and volunteers to execute Javert. When alone with Javert, however, Valjean instead secretly lets him go free. As the army storms the barricade, Valjean grabs the wounded Marius and flees through the sewers. When Valjean emerges hours later, Javert immediately arrests him. Valjean pleads with Javert to let him take the dying Marius to Marius's grandfather. Javert agrees. Javert feels tormented, torn between his duty to his profession and the debt he owes Valjean for saving his life. Ultimately, Javert lets Valjean go and throws himself into the river, where he drowns.

Marius makes a full recovery and is reconciled with Gillenormand, who consents to Marius and Cosette's marriage. Their wedding is a happy one, marred only when Valjean confesses his criminal past to Marius. Alarmed by this revelation and unaware that it was Valjean who saved his life at the barricades, Marius tries to prevent Cosette from having contact with Valjean. Lonely and depressed, Valjean takes to his bed and awaits his death. Marius eventually finds out from Thénardier that Valjean saved Marius's life. Ashamed that he mistrusted Valjean, Marius tells Cosette everything that has happened. Marius and Cosette rush to Valjean's side just in time for a final reconciliation. Happy to be reunited with his adopted daughter, Valjean dies in peace.

CHARACTER LIST

Jean Valjean Cosette's adopted father. Valjean is an ex-convict who leaves behind a life of hatred and deceit and makes his fortune with his innovative industrial techniques. He finds fulfillment in loving his adopted daughter and helping people who are in difficult situations, even when it means risking his own life and welfare. Valjean adopts pseudonyms to evade the police and combines a convict's street smarts with his newfound idealism and compassion. His whole life is a quest for redemption, and he ultimately finds bliss on his deathbed.

Cosette Fantine's daughter, who lives as Valjean's adopted daughter after her mother dies. Cosette spends her childhood as a servant for the Thénardiers in Montfermeil, but even this awful experience does not make her hardened or cynical. Under the care of Valjean and the nuns of Petit-Picpus, Cosette ultimately blossoms into a beautiful, educated young woman. She finds fulfillment in her love for Marius. Cosette is innocent and docile, but her participation in Valjean's many escapes from the law show that she also possesses intelligence and bravery.

Javert A police inspector who strictly believes in law and order and will stop at nothing to enforce France's harsh penal codes. Javert is incapable of compassion or pity, and performs his work with such passion that he takes on a nearly animal quality when he is on the chase. He nurses an especially strong desire to recapture Valjean, whose escapes and prosperity he sees as an affront to justice. Ultimately, Javert is unable to say with certainty that Valjean deserves to be punished. This ambiguity undermines the system of belief on which Javert bases his life and forces him to choose between hypocrisy and honor.

Fantine   A working-class girl who leaves her hometown of Montreuil-sur-mer to seek her fortune in Paris. Fantine's innocent affair with a dapper student named Tholomyès leaves her pregnant and abandoned. Although she is frail, she makes a Herculean effort to feed herself and her daughter, Cosette. Even as she descends into prostitution, she never stops caring for Cosette. She represents the destruction that nineteenth-century French society cruelly wreaks on the less fortunate.

Marius Pontmercy The son of Georges Pontmercy, a colonel in Napoléon's army. Marius grows up in the home of his grandfather, M. Gillenormand, a monarchist. Marius has an identity crisis when he learns the real reason for his separation from his father, and this crisis sets him on the path to discovering himself. An innocent young man, Marius is nonetheless capable of great things and manages both to fight on the barricades and successfully court the love of his life, Cosette.

M. Myriel The bishop of Digne. M. Myriel is a much-admired clergyman whose great kindness and charity have made him popular throughout his parish. He passes on these same qualities to Valjean and initiates the ex-convict's spiritual renewal by saving Valjean from arrest and making him promise to live as an honest man.

M. Thénardier A cruel, wretched, money-obsessed man who first appears as Cosette's keeper and tormentor. Thénardier extorts money from whomever he can, and he frequently serves as an informant to whoever will bid the highest. His schemes range from robbery to fraud to murder, and he has strong ties to the criminal underworld in Paris. Blinded by greed, Thénardier is incapable of loving other human beings and spends every minute in pursuit of money.

Mme. Thénardier M. Thénardier's wife. Mme. Thénardier is just as evil as her husband and takes special pleasure in abusing Cosette. In later years, she becomes her husband's most devoted accomplice and is particularly enthusiastic about his schemes to rob Valjean and Cosette.

Eponine The Thénardiers' eldest daughter. Eponine is a wretched creature who helps her parents steal, but she is eventually redeemed by her love for Marius. She proves that no one is beyond redemption, and she ultimately emerges as one of the novel's most tragic and heroic figures.

M. Gillenormand Marius's ninety-year-old maternal grandfather. Gillenormand prevents Marius from seeing his father, Georges Pontmercy, because he fears that Pontmercy will corrupt Marius. A devout monarchist, Gillenormand rejects the French Revolution outright and also rejects Pontmercy's Napoléonic beliefs. Although Gillenormand's classist views sometimes offend Marius, he truly loves his grandson and ultimately does what is necessary to make Marius happy.

Gavroche The Thénardiers' oldest son. Gavroche is kicked out of the house at an early age and becomes a Parisian street urchin. He is a happy-go-lucky child who enjoys the small pleasures of life and demonstrates unusual generosity toward those even less fortunate than he is. He is also fierce and brave, and plays a decisive role in the barricade even though he does not have a gun.

Colonel Georges Pontmercy An officer in Napoléon's army and Marius's father. Pontmercy is severely wounded at the Battle of Waterloo, and mistakenly believing that Thénardier has saved his life, he asks that Marius honor this debt. Although we know little about Pontmercy's personal life, his politics greatly influence the young Marius.

Enjolras The leader of the Friends of the ABC. Enjolras is a radical student revolutionary. He is both wild and beautiful. Together with Courfeyrac and Marius, Enjolras leads the insurrection at the barricade.

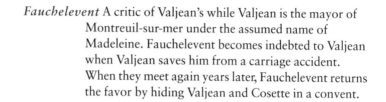

Fauchelevent A critic of Valjean's while Valjean is the mayor of Montreuil-sur-mer under the assumed name of Madeleine. Fauchelevent becomes indebted to Valjean when Valjean saves him from a carriage accident. When they meet again years later, Fauchelevent returns the favor by hiding Valjean and Cosette in a convent.

Petit-Gervais A small boy whom Valjean robs shortly after leaving Digne.

Champmathieu A poor, uneducated man who unfortunately resembles Valjean so much that he is identified, tried, and almost convicted as Valjean. Champmathieu proves to be too dim-witted to defend himself successfully, revealing the callousness of the French justice system.

M. Mabeuf A churchwarden in Paris who tells Marius the truth about his father. Mabeuf and Marius become friends during tough times, and Mabeuf later dies a heroic death on the barricade.

Patron-Minette Actually four people, Patron-Minette is a Parisian crime ring so close-knit that its four members—Montparnasse, Babet, Claquesous, and Gueulemer—are described as four heads of the same violent beast. Patron-Minette controls all the crime in one section of Paris and assists in the Thénardiers' ambush of Valjean.

Felix Tholomyès Fantine's lover in Paris. Tholomyès is a wealthy student who thinks much less of his relationship with Fantine than she does. He gets Fantine pregnant and then abandons her as a joke. Tholomyès is Cosette's biological father, although the two never meet.

Azelma The Thénardiers' younger daughter. Azelma grows up pampered and spoiled but ends up enduring the same poverty as the rest of her family.

ANALYSIS OF MAJOR CHARACTERS

JEAN VALJEAN

Jean Valjean stands at the center of *Les Misérables* and becomes a trial figure for Hugo's grand theories about the redemptive power of compassion and love. Valjean goes into prison a simple and decent man, but his time in jail has a seemingly irreversible effect on him, and he emerges from the chain gang a hardened criminal who hates society for what it has done to him. By the time Valjean encounters M. Myriel in Digne, he is so accustomed to being a social pariah that he almost seeks out such abuse, greeting even the kindly bishop with scorn and hatred. Myriel, however, turns out to be the first person in decades to treat Valjean with love and respect. The meeting with Myriel forever changes Valjean's character, as Myriel makes Valjean promise to become an honest man.

Once Valjean opens up his heart, he becomes a testament to the redemptive power of love and compassion. His hard work and new vision transform the derelict town of Montreuil-sur-mer into a thriving manufacturing center, which in turn teaches Valjean the value of philanthropy. In taking care of Cosette, Valjean learns how to love another person and how to pass that love onto others. He is exceptional only in his physical strength and his willingness to discover what is good, and this earnestness is enough to make him the novel's hero as well as a savior and a friend to a number of people who find themselves in danger. Hardened by prison and rescued by the kindness of M. Myriel, Valjean is a blank slate, molded by his encounters and circumstances. This ability to change makes him a universal symbol of hope—if he can learn love and charity after suffering so much injustice, anyone can.

COSETTE

Cosette, like Valjean, grows up in an atmosphere of poverty and fear, but she is rescued from this life before her innocence gives way to cynicism. Though she spends a number of years under the tyrannical care of the Thénardiers, she never adopts their cruel views, which indicates that she possesses a fundamental decency and goodness that they lack. Once Valjean takes charge of Cosette's upbringing, she quickly transforms from a dirty, unhappy child into a lovely, well-educated young woman. For Hugo, this transformation is so natural that he does not even bother to walk us through it and instead skips several years ahead.

Though she is obedient and fiercely loyal to her adoptive father, Cosette also has her own personality, which emerges as she enters adolescence and begins to hunger for a less sheltered life. In this period of their lives, Valjean's role temporarily changes from Cosette's savior to her jailer. Cosette's ability to truly love Marius, however, is due in large part to Valjean, who has taught her to trust and love. In the end, Cosette remains true to her upbringing, and her love for Marius becomes her way of applying to her own life what she has learned from Valjean.

JAVERT

Javert is so obsessed with enforcing society's laws and morals that he does not realize he is living by mistaken assumptions —a tragic and ironic flaw in a man who believes so strongly in enforcing what he believes is right. Although Javert is such a stern and inflexible character that it is hard to sympathize with him, he lives with the shame of knowing that his own Gypsy upbringing is not so different from the backgrounds of the men he pursues. He lives his life trying to erase this shame through his strict commitment to upholding the law.

Javert's flaw, however, is that he never stops to question whether the laws themselves are just. In his mind, a man is guilty when the law declares him so. When Valjean finally gives Javert irrefutable proof that a man is not necessarily evil just because the law says he is, Javert is incapable of reconciling this new knowledge with his beliefs. He commits suicide, plagued by the thought that he may be living a dishonorable life. True to Javert's nature, he makes this decision not with any emotional hysterics, but rather with a cool determination. Although he is a man of logic, he is impassioned about his work. To this end, Hugo frequently uses animal imagery to describe Javert, particularly when he likens him to a tiger. In the end, it is difficult to feel anything other than pity for Javert, who assumes his duty with such savagery that he seems more animal than man.

MARIUS PONTMERCY

Unlike the other major characters in the novel, Marius grows up in a well-to-do household free of financial worries. Nonetheless, his family is split apart by politics, and it is not until he develops his own personality that he is able to become whole. Marius's loyalties are torn between his father, Georges Pontmercy, who is a colonel in the Napoléonic army, and his staunchly monarchist grandfather, M. Gillenormand, who raises him. The political differences between his father and grandfather threaten to tear apart Marius's identity, as he learns that his conservative grandfather intentionally prevented him from establishing a relationship with his father out of fear that Marius would succumb to his father's liberal political views. Angry and confused, Marius adopts his father's beliefs, but it soon becomes apparent that what he really needs is an idealism of his own. Marius begins to develop truly only when he leaves Gillenormand's house, finding himself and falling in love for the first time.

Marius is more innocent than the other characters in the novel, and while this innocence keeps him from becoming cruel or cynical, it also makes him occasionally blind to the problems of others. This lack of perception first becomes clear in Marius's treatment of Eponine, and becomes especially unattractive when Marius drives Valjean from his house. In the end, Marius is a good person, but his inability to perceive the needs or feeling of others can at times make him unwittingly malicious.

FANTINE

Although all of Fantine's misfortunes are caused by the callousness or greed of others, society always holds her accountable for her behavior. In this sense, she embodies Hugo's view that French society demands the most from those to whom it gives the least. Fantine is a poor, working-class girl from the desolate seacoast town of Montreuil-sur-mer, an orphan who has almost no education and can neither read nor write. Fantine is inevitably betrayed by the people she does trust: Tholomyès gets her pregnant and then disappears; the Thénardiers take Cosette and use the child to extort more money; and Fantine's coworkers have her fired for indecency. In his descriptions of Fantine's life and death, Hugo highlights the unfair attitude of French society toward women and the poor. Fantine's fellow citizens criticize her for her behavior and depravity, but they also take every opportunity to make her circumstances even more desperate.

Hugo's portrayal of Fantine's mistreatment distinguishes the honest, hardworking poor from the parasitic opportunism of the working-class Thénardiers. By juxtaposing Fantine with the Thénardiers, Hugo suggests that poverty does not necessarily equal indecency. In doing so, he condemns a system that allows the indecent poor to survive even as it crushes the honest and needy.

THEMES, MOTIFS & SYMBOLS

THEMES

Themes are the fundamental and often universal ideas explored in a literary work.

THE IMPORTANCE OF LOVE AND COMPASSION

In *Les Misérables,* Hugo asserts that love and compassion are the most important gifts one person can give another and that always displaying these qualities should be the most important goal in life. Valjean's transformation from a hate-filled and hardened criminal into a well-respected philanthropist epitomizes Hugo's emphasis on love, for it is only by learning to love others that Valjean is able to improve himself. While Valjean's efforts on behalf of others inevitably cause him problems, they also give him a sense of happiness and fulfillment that he has never before felt. Valjean's love for others—in particular, for Cosette—is what keeps him going in desperate times.

Hugo also makes clear that loving others, while difficult, is not always a thankless task, and he uses Valjean and Fauchelevent to show that love begets love, and compassion begets compassion. Valjean jumps out of a crowd of onlookers to rescue Fauchelevent; years later, Fauchelevent repays Valjean's bravery by offering him refuge in the convent of Petit-Picpus. In Hugo's novel, love and compassion are nearly infectious, passed on from one person to another. After M. Myriel transforms Valjean with acts of trust and affection, Valjean, in turn, is able to impart this compassion to Cosette, rescuing her from the corrupting cruelty of the Thénardiers. Cosette's love then reaches fulfillment through her marriage to Marius, and their love for each other leads them both to forgive Valjean for his criminal past.

SOCIAL INJUSTICE IN NINETEENTH-CENTURY FRANCE

Hugo uses his novel to condemn the unjust class-based structure of nineteenth-century France, showing time and again that the society's structure turns good, innocent people into beggars and criminals. Hugo focuses on three areas that particularly need reform: education, criminal justice, and the treatment of women. He conveys much of his message through the character of Fantine, a symbol for the many good but impoverished women driven to despair and death by a cruel society. After Fantine is abandoned by her aristocratic lover, Tholomyès, her reputation is indelibly soiled by the fact that she has an illegitimate child. Her efforts to hide this fact are ruined by her lack of education—the scribe to whom Fantine dictates her letters reveals her secret to the whole town. Ironically, it is not until the factory fires Fantine for immorality that she resorts to prostitution. In the character of Fantine, Hugo demonstrates the hypocrisy of a society that fails to educate girls and ostracizes women such as Fantine while encouraging the behavior of men such as Tholomyès .

Hugo casts an even more critical eye on law enforcement. The character of Valjean reveals how the French criminal-justice system transforms a simple bread thief into a career criminal. The only effect of Valjean's nineteen years of mistreatment on the chain gang is that he becomes sneaky and vicious—a sharp contrast to the effect of Myriel's kindness, which sets Valjean on the right path almost overnight. Another contrast to Valjean's plight is the selective manner in which the Parisian police deal with the Patron-Minette crime ring. Unlike Valjean, Patron-Minette and their associates are real criminals who rob and murder on a grand scale, but they receive only short sentences in prisons that are easy to escape. In the French society of *Les Misérables,* therefore, justice is clumsy at best. It barely punishes the worst criminals but tears apart the lives of people who commit petty crimes.

THE LONG-TERM EFFECTS OF THE FRENCH REVOLUTION ON FRENCH SOCIETY

In *Les Misérables,* Hugo traces the social impact of the numerous revolutions, insurrections, and executions that took place in late eighteenth- and early nineteenth-century France. By chronicling the rise and fall of Napoléon as well as the restoration and subsequent decline of the Bourbon monarchy, Hugo gives us a sense of the perpetual uncertainty that political events imposed upon daily life. Though Hugo's sympathies are with republican movements rather than with the monarchy, he criticizes all of the regimes since the French Revolution of 1789 for their inability to deal effectively with social injustice or eliminate France's rigid class system. Hugo describes the Battle of Waterloo, for instance, in glowing terms, but reminds us that at the end of the glorious battle, the old blights of society, like the grave robbers, still remain. Similarly, the battle at the barricade is both heroic and futile—a few soldiers are killed, but the insurgents are slaughtered without achieving anything. The revolution that Hugo champions is a moral one, in which the old system of greed and corruption is replaced by one of compassion. Although both Napoléon and the students at the barricade come closer to espousing these values than the French monarchs do, these are not values than can be imposed through violence. Indeed, Hugo shows that Napoléon and the students at the barricades topple as easily as the monarchy.

MOTIFS

Motifs are recurring structures, contrasts, or literary devices that can help to develop and inform the text's major themes.

THE PLIGHT OF THE ORPHAN

The prevalence of orphans and unusual family structures in *Les Misérables* is the most obvious indicator that French society and politics in the period described have gone terribly wrong. Valjean, Fantine, Cosette, Marius, Gavroche, Pontmercy, and Gillenormand are all separated from their family or loved ones for economic or political reasons. Marius embodies the disastrous effects of politics on family structure, torn as he is between Gillenormand's monarchism and Pontmercy's embrace of Napoléon. Social instability and poverty, meanwhile, make orphans of Cosette, Valjean, Fantine, and Gavroche. With the exception of Gavroche, whose home life is so wretched that he is probably better off on his own, these characters are unhappy and lonely because they are separated from their parents and have no one to turn to when they most need help.

DISGUISES AND PSEUDONYMS

A number of characters in the novel operate under pseudonyms or in disguise, and these deliberate changes in identity become the distinctive mark of the criminal world. Thénardier is a prime example: at one point in the novel, he masquerades under the name Jondrette, and we see that he has adopted other pseudonyms at the same time. Valjean, who uses pseudonyms to hide his past rather than to continue his criminal behavior, inhabits his alter egos more thoroughly.

Even Valjean's disguises, while not as dishonorable as Thénardier's, are an unfulfilling way of living, and the first thing Valjean does after Cosette's marriage is shed his fake name in front of his new family. Disguises and pseudonyms are a means of survival for the novel's characters, but Hugo believes that life is about more than mere survival. Ultimately, one of the most important distinctions between the honest characters and the criminals is the willingness of the honest characters to set aside their alter egos and reveal themselves for who they truly are.

RESURRECTION

When a character in *Les Misérables* learns a major lesson about life, this realization is often accompanied by a physical resurrection. Valjean undergoes the largest number of reincarnations, each of which denotes that he is another step away from his old moral depravity. After his encounter with Myriel, for instance, Valjean reinvents himself as Madeleine, and he leaves this identity behind when he pretends to drown in the waters of Toulon. The epitome of this resurrection motif is the ruse with the coffin that Valjean devises in order to remain at the convent of Petit-Picpus. Valjean is not the only one to undergo such resurrections, however. When Marius finally recovers six months after being wounded at the barricades, he is a different man from the love-stricken suitor who goes to fight. Although he does not assume a new identity, Marius needs to experience a metaphorical death before he can reconcile himself with his grandfather and successfully court Cosette.

SYMBOLS

Symbols are objects, characters, figures, or colors used to represent abstract ideas or concepts.

MYRIEL'S SILVER CANDLESTICKS

M. Myriel's candlesticks are the most prominent symbol of compassion in *Les Misérables,* and they shed a light that always brings love and hope. At the beginning of the novel, Hugo uses the contrast between light and darkness to underscore the differences between Myriel, an upstanding citizen, and Valjean, a dark, brooding figure seemingly incapable of love. When Myriel gives Valjean his silver candlesticks, Myriel is literally passing on this light as he tells Valjean he must promise to become an honest man. Subsequently, the candlesticks reappear frequently to remind Valjean of his duty. When Valjean dies, the candlesticks shine brightly across his face, a symbolic affirmation that he has attained his goal of love and compassion.

Snakes, Insects, and Birds

When describing the novel's main characters, Hugo uses animal imagery to accentuate these characters' qualities of good and evil. The orphaned figures of Cosette and Gavroche are frequently referred to as creatures of flight: Cosette as a lark and Gavroche as a fly. The Thénardiers, on the other hand, are described as snakes, and Cosette's time among them is likened to living with beetles. These opposing symbols suggest that whereas Cosette and Gavroche can rise above their miserable circumstances, the Thénardiers are rooted in their immoral pursuits. They are creatures of the earth, which means that they are not as free as Cosette or Gavroche, who can fly wherever they please.

Summary & Analysis

"Fantine," Books One–Two

Summary: Book One: An Upright Man

The novel begins with a brief biography of M. Myriel, the bishop of Digne, a diocese in France. Born in 1740 to a wealthy aristocratic family, Myriel is forced to flee to Italy during the French Revolution of 1789. Years later, he returns to his homeland as a priest. A chance encounter with Emperor Napoléon in 1806 leads to Myriel's appointment as bishop of Digne. When he moves to Digne, he discovers that the church has provided him and his small entourage with a well-appointed eighteenth-century palace, while the patients at the hospital next door live in cramped and dangerous conditions. Myriel insists on switching houses with the hospital and gives the majority of his church salary to the city's poorest citizens and to charities in Paris and abroad.

Myriel and his family live a simple life, but out of consideration for his housekeeper, he holds on to two little luxuries: a set of silverware and two silver candlesticks. Myriel's compassion earns him the love of his parishioners, and he becomes a clergyman of wide renown. He defends the needs of the poor and argues that most petty criminals steal to survive, not because they are inherently malicious. He becomes a vocal critic of the prejudices of French society and an advocate for universal education. Among the needy, Myriel's actions earn him the nickname "Bienvenu," which means "welcome."

Summary: Book Two: The Fall

> *[Valjean's] knees suddenly bent under him. . . . [H]e*
> *fell exhausted . . . and cried out, "I'm such a miserable*
> *man!"* (See QUOTATIONS, p. 65)

In October 1815, a mysterious wanderer enters Digne. The man has been walking all day and is desperately hungry. His first stop is at the mayor's office, where the law requires him to show a yellow passport indicating that he is an ex-convict. The man is tired and hungry, but the town's innkeepers refuse to serve him. He tries the town prison, the houses of local villagers, and even a dog kennel, but his reputation has preceded him and the townspeople are afraid. When the stranger stops at Myriel's house, however, the bishop immediately invites him in for dinner.

The stranger's name is Jean Valjean, a tree-trimmer from the south of France who has spent the last nineteen years in prison. The first five years of Valjean's prison term were for stealing a loaf of bread to feed his impoverished family, and the next fourteen were imposed for his frequent escape attempts. He is used to rough treatment and is surprised by the respect Myriel shows him. Valjean does not initially realize that Myriel is a member of the clergy and is certainly not aware that he is a bishop. Myriel invites Valjean to spend the night free of charge. He accepts the invitation but then leaves in the night with Myriel's silverware.

Early the next day, the police stop Valjean. They discover the silverware in his knapsack and take him back to Myriel's house. To everyone's surprise, Myriel claims that he gave the silverware to Valjean and even chides Valjean for having forgotten to take the silver candlesticks as well. Valjean is immediately released. Myriel gives Valjean the candlesticks and tells him that in taking the candlesticks, he has made a promise to become an honest man.

Humiliated and confused, Valjean leaves town furtively, as if he were still on the run. In the countryside, he takes a silver coin from a little boy named Petit Gervais. As the boy runs off crying, Valjean is struck by the wickedness of his act. He tries in vain to find the boy and return the coin. Valjean begins to cry for the first time in nineteen years. Confronted by his own malice, he vows to become an upstanding citizen. Later that night, he prays on the doorstep of Myriel's house.

ANALYSIS: BOOKS ONE–TWO

Personal change figures prominently in the first few chapters of *Les Misérables,* as Hugo uses Myriel and Valjean to demonstrate that change is a vital part of human nature. On the one hand, Hugo uses Myriel to show the positive effects of change. Myriel leaves for Italy as a spoiled aristocrat but returns as a clergyman who lives in simple piety. He is no longer preoccupied with material pleasures, and his new interest in the welfare of others makes him as happy as it makes those who receive his care. With the character of Myriel, Hugo expresses his optimism in an individual's ability to improve, rejecting the fatalistic notion that individuals are born with character traits that cannot be altered.

In contrast, Hugo uses Valjean to make the point that preventing people from developing for the better can destroy them. Valjean does not come into the town as a thief, but his yellow passport immediately brands him as an undesirable character. Consequently, the townspeople are openly hostile toward him and refuse to believe that he is capable of anything other than theft. The townspeople have such an unyielding and rigid view of Valjean that he comes to believe it himself. Valjean does not need to steal Myriel's silver, but he does so largely because the town expects such criminality of him.

Hugo makes the contrast between Myriel and Valjean clear through visual imagery, referring to the men in terms of light and dark. Myriel, who trusts in and hopes for other people, operates in light, whereas the mistrustful Valjean operates in darkness. The tension between light and dark reaches a peak when Valjean stops to look at Myriel before stealing his silver. As Valjean plans his theft, the clouds darken the sky; he then sees Myriel's face in a beam of moonlight. Finally, we see Valjean standing in the shadows while he breaks into the cabinet of silver. In this description, Hugo uses a literary device called pathetic fallacy, a technique in which a nonhuman entity—in this case, nature—takes on human attitudes or traits to accentuate the tension between good and bad. As Valjean contemplates stealing the silver, the sky is dark, as if it were frowning upon the crime he is about to commit. Once Valjean approaches Myriel, however, everything becomes light, as if Myriel were radiating purity and goodness. By using this technique of pathetic fallacy, Hugo is able to pass judgment on his characters and their actions without ever breaking the narrative voice.

Hugo's dissatisfaction with certain social institutions becomes apparent in these early chapters when he uses Valjean's imprisonment to show the inadequacy and ineptitude of France's prison systems. Valjean is arrested simply for stealing a loaf of bread to feed his starving family, only to emerge from prison nineteen years later tougher and more ruthless than he was when he entered. We cannot blame this failure on Valjean's nature, since we see that just a single night at Myriel's house is enough to change him. Therefore, the fault lies with the prison system. Indeed, Hugo's brief descriptions of the prison in which he stayed are so brutal that we sympathize with Valjean's frequent attempts to escape. Hugo advocates compassion rather than this harsh prison treatment. Myriel's kindness does not have immediate results, but it activates Valjean's conscience, causing him to cry over the evil that has overtaken his soul and to make his first steps to atone for his deeds.

"FANTINE," BOOKS THREE–FOUR

SUMMARY: BOOK THREE: THE YEAR 1817

The next section of the novel takes place in 1817, two years after Myriel gives the candlesticks to Valjean. The narrator provides a quick sketch of contemporary Parisian politics, culture, and art, and then introduces four well-to-do university students named Tholomyès, Listolier, Fameuil, and Blacheville. The four are good friends, and all have mistresses who come from the working or lower-middle classes. The youngest of these four young women is Fantine, an orphan raised by the state. Whereas the other women are more experienced in the ways of the world, Fantine falls head over heels in love with Tholomyès and makes him her first lover.

One day, Tholomyès proposes to the other four men that they play a trick on their mistresses. The following Sunday, the students invite the women out to dinner, then announce that they must leave to prepare a surprise. The women are excited, but their pleasure turns to chagrin when the waiter brings them a sealed envelope. Inside they find a letter, signed by all four men, in which the men announce that their parents will no longer allow them to consort with working-class women. The three older women do not seem surprised, and Fantine pretends to laugh along with them. In reality, however, she is heartbroken, all the more so since she is pregnant with Tholomyès's child.

SUMMARY: BOOK FOUR:
TO TRUST IS SOMETIMES TO SURRENDER

A few years pass. Fantine decides that she can best support her daughter, Cosette, in her hometown of Montreuil-sur-mer. She leaves Paris, but realizes that she will be unable to work in Montreuil if the townspeople discover that she has an illegitimate daughter. She stops at an inn to rest and consider what to do next. While resting, Fantine sees two girls playing happily in front of a tavern. She makes conversation with their mother, a woman named Madame Thénardier. Fantine eventually begs Mme. Thénardier to look after Cosette while Fantine looks for work. At this point, Monsieur Thénardier intervenes, demanding that Fantine send money to the Thénardiers every month in return for looking after Cosette. Fantine is reluctant to leave Cosette, but she is comforted by the thought that her daughter will be in good hands.

The Thénardiers, however, turn out to be swindlers. They force Cosette to perform heavy household work, dress her in rags, and frequently beat her. The Thénardiers use the money Fantine sends to cover their own expenses, and they pawn Cosette's clothing. When Thénardier discovers that Cosette is an illegitimate child, he begins to demand more and more money from Fantine.

ANALYSIS: BOOKS THREE–FOUR

Hugo gives Book Three a very theatrical feel, using fast-paced dialogue and humor to show us how overwhelmed Fantine is by her surroundings. Though Fantine emerges as a major character in the novel, Hugo's emphasis on spoken dialogue in this section prevents us from recognizing Fantine's importance immediately, since Fantine is often so silent that we can easily forget she is there. A humorous tone dominates this section and reinforces our sense of Fantine's naïveté. She often does not understand when her companions are joking and therefore does not realize that her relationship with Tholomyès is the biggest joke of all. Instead, Fantine takes Tholomyès's promises of love as earnestly as she takes his jokes, and she gives herself completely to him. The ways in which Hugo uses humor and dialogue makes his prose read almost like a play, with Fantine as a simple spectator who does not fully understand the action unfolding in front of her. The four students view life as a comedy, and they are too callous and selfish to care that Fantine has mistaken their idle jests for sincere emotions.

Hugo further satirizes the middle class through his depiction of the Thénardiers. Unlike the idly rich students who abuse and abandon women like Fantine, the Thénardiers do work for a living. However, the fact that they earn their keep does not make them sympathetic. Without any trace of scruples or remorse, the Thénardiers enslave Cosette and force her trusting mother to pay more and more money for their own amusements, denying Cosette any benefits from these payments. The Thénardiers' only goal is to make as much money as possible while doing as little work as they can. In this respect, they are simply a poorer version of the aristocrats. The

Thénardiers are far lower on the social ladder than Tholomyès, but they exploit Fantine more ruthlessly than he does.

There are echoes of *Cinderella,* the Grimm fairy tale, in the relationship between the Thénardiers and Cosette, which Hugo uses to comment on the role mothers play in the development of their daughters. While Thénardier plays a more prominent role later in the novel, most of Cosette's maltreatment actually comes at the hands of Mme. Thénardier and her two daughters, Eponine and Azelma—Hugo's interpretation of the evil stepmother and evil stepsisters, respectively. Hugo notes that "[Madame Thénardier] was unkind to Cosette and Eponine and Azelma were unkind, too. Children at that age are simply copies of the mother; only the size is reduced." Here, Hugo identifies the mother as the most important factor in determining a child's development and suggests that Cosette's upbringing is impaired because Fantine is absent.

The relationship between parents and children, which is emphasized throughout the novel, surfaces in the letter that Tholomyès and his friends leave their mistresses. In their letter, the four students write, "Understand, we have parents. Parents—you barely know the meaning of the word," indicating that Fantine and the other working-class girls come from broken homes. Here, Hugo points to the breakdown of the traditional family among the working class, a dissolution brought about by the struggle to survive. These instances of ruptured family relations—of orphans, unwanted children, and foster parents—represent Hugo's comment on the upturned social order and broken family ties that he felt plagued the working classes of early nineteenth-century France.

"FANTINE," BOOK FIVE: THE DESCENT

SUMMARY

Twelve years have passed since Fantine has been to her hometown of Montreuil-sur-mer, and she is surprised at how much the town has grown and modernized during the past decade. The changes are largely due to Monsieur Madeleine, a stranger about whom little is known. The narrator says that Madeleine arrived in Montreuil in 1815 with a newer, cheaper method for producing black beads, the town's largest industry. A manufacturing revolution ensued, and Madeleine's cunning and philanthropy so impressed the king that he made Madeleine the mayor of Montreuil in 1820. No one knows much about Madeleine's past, but he has been wildly popular since the day he saved two local children from a fire. The townspeople do not, therefore, comment on Madeleine's quirks and foibles, such as his wearing of a black hatband after the death of the bishop Myriel.

Only Javert, the town's police inspector, suspects that Madeleine may be harboring a dark secret. Javert suspects that Madeleine is actually Jean Valjean, an extraordinarily strong convict whom Javert once guarded. Javert's suspicions are heightened when he witnesses Madeleine rescue a man, Fauchelevent, by lifting him from underneath a fallen carriage. Though Madeleine is aware of Javert's suspicions, he does not appear to feel threatened by them.

Fantine finds employment in Madeleine's factory, but her secretive manner makes her coworkers suspicious. The illiterate Fantine writes letters to the Thénardiers by dictating to a scribe who turns out to be a gossip and who tells the factory workers that Fantine is hiding an illegitimate child. Fantine is subsequently fired from her job on charges of immorality. She owes many people money, and although she tries to live on as little as she can, the Thénardiers continue to raise their price for taking care of Cosette. To satisfy their demands, Fantine first sells her hair, then her front teeth, and finally, becomes a prostitute. Nonetheless, Thénardier threatens to kick Cosette out if Fantine does not pay him one hundred francs.

One night, a man harasses Fantine as she waits for potential clients outside a bar. The man hits Fantine with a snowball, and she snaps and attacks him. Javert arrests Fantine and threatens her with six months in jail, ignoring her pleas that he think of her child and show mercy. Madeleine intervenes, freeing Fantine and promising to take care of her and Cosette. Fantine, who blames Madeleine for firing her, spits in his face. Madeleine does not flinch and repeats his offer of help. Fantine is so overwhelmed by Madeleine's kindness that she faints. Javert is outraged that Madeleine has overruled his decision and decides to investigate Madeleine's past.

ANALYSIS

Hugo's focus on Montreuil-sur-mer's new prosperity shows his enthusiasm for the Industrial Revolution. He depicts the Industrial Revolution as nothing short of miraculous, a time when a few simple changes in manufacturing technique can rejuvenate an entire region. By having Madeleine revolutionize a traditional industry, Hugo preemptively counters the argument that industrial development comes at the expense of tradition. He links Madeleine's prosperity with his philanthropy and the success of his factories. Hugo believes that technology levels the playing field, creating a world where what is good for one is good for all, where even a passing stranger can make a fortune. Madeleine seems to be a man with no past and no connections, but this apparent lack of background makes no difference in the world of the Industrial Revolution. Unlike the characters in class-conscious Paris and Digne, Madeleine prospers and thrives by using his brains.

In his enthusiasm for the Industrial Revolution, Hugo reverses his usual perspective by focusing on a hero, Madeleine, who is a prosperous man. Hugo continues to champion the rights of the poor and oppressed, but in Book Five the workers are responsible for bringing most of their misery upon one another. Fantine's misfortunes and descent into prostitution are caused by the nosiness of her fellow workers—not, as she suspects, by any cruelty on Madeleine's part. Hugo still criticizes the upper classes—the man whom Fantine assaults is a bourgeois dandy—but he makes the hero of these chapters the town's wealthiest man. In contrast to other novels set during the Industrial Revolution, in which factory bosses are often portrayed as brutal, heartless, and greedy, in *Les Misérables* it is the boss who helps the poor escape the injustices of outdated social hierarchies. While this sympathetic portrayal of the wealthy industrialist does not contradict the message of Hugo's earlier chapters, it is a surprise from an author whose sympathies are usually with the poor.

Hugo uses foreshadowing in these chapters, dropping multiple hints that Madeleine is in fact Jean Valjean. He helps us interpret these clues through Javert's unwavering eyes. The narrator notes, for example, that no one thinks to ask Madeleine for his passport because his rescue of two children has made him an unquestioned hero. The narrator also casually mentions that Madeleine wears a black armband upon hearing of Myriel's death, which we know is something Valjean might do since Myriel is so important to him. In case we miss some of these hints about Valjean's true nature, Hugo provides Javert's investigative eye to interpret them for us. Though we might not, for instance, understand the significance of Madeleine's rescue of Fauchelevent, Javert immediately notes this act as a sign that Madeleine possesses Valjean's unusual strength. These clues make us fairly sure that Madeleine is indeed Valjean. However, like Javert, we do not have proof, and we begin to anticipate the climactic moment when our suspicions will be confirmed.

"Fantine," Books Six–Eight

Summary: Book Six: Javert

Fantine develops a chronic chest ailment. As her condition worsens, Madeleine continues to care for her. Madeleine also sends money to the Thénardiers, but they realize that it would be more profitable for them to hold on to Cosette, so they refuse to send her to Fantine. Madeleine plans to retrieve Cosette, but his plan is derailed when Javert visits him and demands to be fired. Javert tells Madeleine that he has long suspected him of being Valjean and that he denounced Madeleine after the mayor ordered Fantine's release. Javert claims that he has since discovered that Valjean, pretending to be a man named Champmathieu, has just been rearrested for robbery and is standing trial in the town of Arras. Javert claims that he has positively identified Champmathieu as Valjean and that he is leaving for Arras to testify in the trial the following day. Madeleine pretends to be unconcerned and refuses to relieve Javert of his duties.

Summary: Book Seven: The Champmathieu Affair

Madeleine, who is Valjean in disguise, is faced with the agonizing decision of whether to turn himself in. If he reveals his true identity, the innocent Champmathieu will be freed, but Valjean will no longer be able to help the poor people of Montreuil-sur-mer. Valjean decides to stay and burns any clothes and personal effects that could prove his true identity. When he sees the coin he stole from Petit Gervais, however, Valjean recalls the promise he made to Myriel to become an honest man. After agonizing for the whole night, Valjean finally gives in to his conscience and decides to go to the trial in Arras.

A number of mishaps delay Madeleine, and by the time he arrives in Arras he is convinced that he is too late. A guard tries to stop Madeleine from entering the courtroom, but his fame and widespread respect precede him, and he enters the courtroom through a secret door reserved for honored guests. To Madeleine's horror, he discovers that Champmathieu does resemble him but that the man is not smart enough to defend himself properly. Javert has already given his testimony, and three of Valjean's former prison mates swear that Champmathieu is in fact Valjean. Just as Champmathieu is about to be convicted, Madeleine interrupts the trial and reveals that he is Valjean.

SUMMARY: BOOK EIGHT: COUNTER-STROKE

The court exonerates Champmathieu. In the confusion that ensues, Valjean has time to return to Montreuil-sur-mer and help Fantine. Javert appears, visibly excited by the prospect of arresting Valjean. Valjean begs Javert to go and retrieve Cosette from the Thénardiers, but Javert only laughs at him. Fantine, horrified by the news that her daughter is not yet in Montreuil, dies of shock. Valjean angrily breaks free from Javert's grasp, blaming him for Fantine's death. He whispers something in Fantine's ear. Later that night, Valjean breaks out of jail and returns home to organize his affairs. He leaves his fortune to the poor and heads for Paris. Fantine is buried in a public grave.

ANALYSIS: BOOKS SIX–EIGHT

Valjean 's decision to reveal his identity is an agonizing one, since he knows that both admission and concealment will have huge consequences. Hugo appropriately titles the chapter in which Valjean makes his decision "A Tempest within a Brain," revealing how torturous this choice is. The two perspectives argue with each other within Valjean's mind, and he hears so many different voices that the chapter almost feels like a bout of schizophrenia. Valjean's desire to exonerate Champmathieu is laudable, but doing so would be, in his thinking, an act of egotism: since the entire town has come to depend on Valjean's business and philanthropy, he would be abandoning many people who count on him if he turned himself in to satisfy his own guilt. On the other hand, Valjean's belief that the needs of many outweigh the needs of the few conflicts with the promise he makes to Myriel.

Though Hugo spends time exploring Valjean's heart-wrenching dilemma, Hugo's main objective in this section is to critique the French criminal-justice system. We have already seen Myriel criticize capital punishment and the failure of incarceration to rehabilitate convicts. Hugo now takes this critique a step further by attacking the credibility of the courts. Valjean publicly denounces the prisons for turning average men into hardened criminals, and Champmathieu's trial is an absurdity that calls into question the validity of the entire court. The prosecution's case depends upon the statements of four unreliable witnesses—three convicts and Javert, who is too obsessed with catching Valjean to be objective. The prosecution is too clumsy to convict Champmathieu for his original crime of stealing apples.

The only reason the trial proceeds is because Champmathieu is not smart enough to defend himself or understand what is going on. Hugo describes the walls of the courtroom as dirty and stained, a symbol of the corrupt court system. Champmathieu's trial compares unfavorably to Valjean's own deliberations of the night before, which were far more tortuous but also fundamentally more decent and honest.

"COSETTE," BOOKS ONE–TWO

SUMMARY: BOOK ONE: WATERLOO

It is June 18, 1815, and the narrator gives us a vivid and extensive account of the Battle of Waterloo. This battle marks the defeat of Napoléon Bonaparte and the end of his empire. The narrator, suggesting that most accounts of the battle are seen from the perspective of the victorious British, resolves to focus instead on the efforts of the French forces. Napoléon's men view their leader with "religious awe," but despite his brilliance they are defeated by foul weather. Napoléon has more artillery than Wellington, the British commander, but a sudden rainstorm delays the battle and gives Prussian reinforcements time to arrive and help the British. The French get stuck in an impassable muddy road and are wiped out by British artillery. Though the French are defeated, the narrator claims that the real victors of Waterloo are the individual men who are standing up for their beliefs. He cites the heroic example of Cambronne, a soldier who, when called upon by the British to surrender, stubbornly fights to his death.

During the night following the battle, prowlers emerge and begin to steal gold and jewelry from the dead soldiers. This pursuit is dangerous, since the leader of the English troops has ordered all thieves to be shot dead. As one prowler steals a cross, a watch, and money from a seemingly dead officer, the officer suddenly revives. The officer thinks the prowler has saved his life and asks his name. The robber replies that his name is Thénardier. The officer, whose name is Georges Pontmercy, promises always to remember Thénardier for saving his life.

SUMMARY: BOOK TWO: THE SHIP ORION

Rumors fly about the capture of Jean Valjean. Newspaper articles suggest he was Fantine's lover and that he withdrew 700,000 francs just before his arrest. In the town of Montfermeil, where the Thénardiers' inn is located, people notice an old road-mender named Boulatruelle digging holes in the forest. Thénardier gets Boulatruelle drunk. The old man reveals that he has seen former prison comrade enter the forest with a small chest, a pick, and a shovel, and that he is trying to find the buried treasure.

The narrator directs our attention to a newspaper article about the *Orion*, a warship docked in Toulon. In November 1823, a sailor on the *Orion* falls off one the ship's masts, barely catching hold of a footrope. No one from the substantial crowd is willing to make the dangerous effort to rescue the sailor, but one of the convicts on the ship's chain gang asks for permission to rescue the man. The officer agrees and the prisoner climbs up the ship's rigging and saves the sailor. The crowd applauds the prisoner's death-defying feat, but the prisoner suddenly stumbles and falls into the water. He does not resurface. After an extensive search, the convict, who is Jean Valjean, is proclaimed drowned.

ANALYSIS: BOOKS ONE–TWO

Valor and heroism are the dominant qualities in this section, as Hugo contrasts the valiant behavior of the French army with the dishonorable actions of Thénardier in order to draw a distinction between real heroes and false ones. Thénardier is less savory than the rest of the army, a person so despicable that the English commander orders men like him shot without trial. Ironically, however, Thénardier is the man whom Pontmercy mistakenly identifies as a hero. Hugo does not dispute that real heroes exist, since he greatly admires the defiant Cambronne, who soldiers on against all odds. By introducing Thénardier at the end of the account of Waterloo, however, Hugo reveals that not all heroes are what they seem; Pontmercy's gratitude toward Thénardier suggests that some men we regard as heroes may in fact be scoundrels. Hugo also implies that men who usurp the title of hero bring shame upon everyone else, as the description of Thénardier's graveyard prowling interrupts Hugo's rousing historical account of Waterloo and causes it to end on a disgraceful note.

The idea of real and false heroes extends beyond the episode at Waterloo and allows us to view Thénardier as a foil (a character whose behavior or personality underscores opposing traits in another character) for Valjean. Like Cambronne and the rest of the soldiers who die at Waterloo, Valjean is brave, determined, and conscientious. We see his heroism all the more clearly when we compare it to the despicable behavior of Thénardier, who robs the dead and falsely takes credit for bravery that he does not actually exhibit. Valjean clearly possesses more admirable qualities, but it is Thénardier who is erroneously rewarded for his actions. Hugo encapsulates the flaws in society's values by contrasting these two men's intentions with the unfair ways in which they are rewarded. While Thénardier's lies earn him glory and gratitude, Valjean's true heroism earns him persecution and jail time.

The fact that Hugo interprets Waterloo as a defeat for France due to bad luck shows us that unfairness and injustice are not limited to the world of Valjean but have a part in larger events as well. Hugo views Napoléon as a brilliant strategist and a defender of equality who brings France to new heights. Nonetheless, Napoléon loses at Waterloo. Even worse, according to Hugo, is the fact that Napoléon loses the battle because of something as banal as the weather, not because of any substantive blunders on his part or any significant ingenuity on the part of the British. The defeat at Waterloo is as arbitrary and unfair as Valjean's imprisonment, but on a larger scale. The unfair outcomes leave us hungry for justice, anticipating the unrest that emerges in later chapters.

Stylistically, the battle accounts and fictitious newspaper excerpts are a departure from Hugo's straightforward narrative style. These devices emphasize the fact that though Hugo's characters are fictional, the novel's plot turns on actual events in the history of France. The change in narrative mode also lends dynamism to the novel by including a number of different perspectives.

SUMMARY & ANALYSIS

"COSETTE," BOOK THREE: FULFILLMENT OF THE PROMISE MADE TO THE DEPARTED

SUMMARY

> *At that moment [Cosette] suddenly felt that the weight of the bucket was gone.*
>
> (See QUOTATIONS, p. 66)

The novel reintroduces us to Cosette on Christmas Eve of 1823, one month after Valjean disappears in the waters of Toulon. She is now eight years old and still lives with the Thénardiers in Montfermeil. They force Cosette to work, beat her, insult her mother, and practically starve her, while pampering and spoiling their own two daughters, Eponine and Azelma. But they treat their baby boy, Gavroche, as poorly as Cosette, viewing him as merely another mouth to feed.

A group of travelers arrive at the inn, and Mme. Thénardier orders Cosette to go to the woods to fetch a bucket of water. Cosette is terrified of going into the woods at night and tries to delay, but Mme. Thénardier screams at her to hurry. The forest is dark, cold, and terrifying, and when Cosette fills the bucket, she can barely carry it. She cries out to God. Out of nowhere, a large hand reaches down and lifts the bucket from her shoulders. Though Cosette does not know her rescuer, she is remarkably not afraid of the large man holding the bucket.

The man, who is Valjean, is surprised to learn that this girl is Cosette. He follows her back to the Thénardiers' inn, where he intends to spend the night. Valjean is shocked to see how Cosette is treated at the inn, and he throws money around to persuade the Thénardiers to let her enjoy Christmas Eve. The Thénardiers realize that their guest is wealthy and begin to treat him better. They are particularly astonished when he steps out into the street and returns with an expensive doll as a gift for Cosette.

The next morning, Valjean asks the Thénardiers to give him Cosette. Mme. Thénardier jumps at the opportunity, but M. Thénardier pretends to be reluctant to part with the girl, hoping to gouge more money out of Valjean. Without haggling, Valjean pays Thénardier 1,500 francs and leaves with Cosette. Thénardier runs after them to demand more money. He says he cannot give away Cosette without permission from her mother, and Valjean produces the note from Fantine. Thénardier argues, but when he notices Valjean's physical size, he decides it is more prudent to let the matter go. Safe at last, Cosette falls asleep in Valjean's arms.

ANALYSIS

Valjean has been a noble figure since his redemption, but in this section he comes across as almost saintly, particularly when contrasted with the Thénardiers. Significantly, Valjean arrives in Montfermeil on Christmas Eve and seizes Cosette's bucket at the exact moment that she cries out to God—details that make his entrance seem divine. The idea that Valjean is Cosette's savior is reinforced by his selfless generosity. He pays money so that Cosette can take time off on Christmas Eve, and when Thénardier demands 1,500 francs to release Cosette, Valjean pays the sum without hesitation. The fact that Valjean does not haggle may come across as implausibly passive—after all, there is no reason why he cannot be compassionate but still bargain. Yet it becomes more understandable when we see Thénardier's greedy maneuvering for the best price. Thénardier may be skilled at getting a material bargain, but his willingness to sell a child and haggle over the price shows that he is spiritually bankrupt.

Hugo's disdain for materialism pervades his descriptions of the Thénardiers' tavern. The detailed descriptions of the couple's belongings and of the various ways in which they cheat others reveal how thoroughly their lives are dominated by the quest for money and possessions. The Thénardiers' pursuit of material goods leads them to engage in an unending series of immoral acts, from tax evasion to child slavery. The fact that the Thénardiers regard their third child as little more than a drain on household finances further underscores their greed. Despite all of these schemes, the Thénardiers never feel as if they have enough cash—their love of money verges on an addiction.

Hugo proposes love as the antidote to such materialism, and the moment when Valjean takes Cosette in his arms demonstrates Hugo's belief that love enriches all parties involved. Indeed, Hugo stresses the importance of love above all other emotions. Although Valjean's arrival heralds a new sense of safety for Cosette, it is not until he actually takes her in his arms that she feels whole. Love transforms Valjean's quest from a simple rescue mission into something true and fulfilling. His life is still missing something, especially since helping others has so far been a thankless task. When Valjean picks up Cosette, however, he discovers that good deeds can bring the joy of being loved. His previous actions made him content, but his love for Cosette makes him supremely happy, beginning the second and final stage of his spiritual transformation.

"COSETTE," BOOKS FOUR–FIVE

SUMMARY: BOOK FOUR: THE OLD GORBEAU HOUSE

Valjean finds an out-of-the-way place where he and Cosette can live —a rundown tenement called the Gorbeau House. Valjean tells the landlady that Cosette is his granddaughter. He soon acquires a reputation in the neighborhood for philanthropy, and because his own clothes are so shoddy, the locals call him the "beggar who gives alms." One day, Valjean stops to give a beggar some money and is petrified when he sees what he thinks is Javert's face peering out from under the beggar's hood. Valjean has heard rumors that the beggar is a police spy, but he assures himself that he is imagining things.

The next night, Valjean hears the sound of unfamiliar footsteps coming up the stairs of his tenement. He tells Cosette to keep absolutely silent and stays up all night waiting for the person outside their apartment to leave. Toward daybreak, Valjean hears someone heading back downstairs. Valjean peers through the keyhole and sees the unmistakable figure of Javert. Later that morning, the landlady asks Valjean if he heard anyone come in during the previous evening. Valjean replies that he heard footsteps, and the landlady tells him it was probably the new tenant, a man named Dumont. Valjean begins to worry that the landlady is spying on him for Javert. He resolves to leave the Gorbeau House as quickly as possible.

BOOK FIVE: A DARK CHASE REQUIRES A SILENT HOUND

Valjean hurriedly packs all of his and Cosette's belongings and they rush out of the apartment as soon as it is dark. Valjean senses that they are being followed and sees Javert and two other policemen close behind them. With Cosette in his arms, Valjean runs across the eastern quarters of Paris for hours, but he is unable to shake Javert completely. After crossing the river Seine on the Austerlitz Bridge, Valjean is confident that he is finally free. He soon sees, however, that Javert is still close behind and that the number of men with him has grown.

Without hesitation, Valjean rushes down a dark alleyway, only to realize that it is a dead end. Peering around the corner of the alley, he sees that Javert has commandeered a passing patrol and that they are at most fifteen minutes away from finding him. Desperate, Valjean decides to draw on his old talent for climbing, a skill that he mastered as a convict. To persuade Cosette to go along with his desperate plan, he tells her that the Thénardiers are after them. By a stroke of luck, he finds a length of rope attached to a nearby lamppost. He cuts the rope down and attaches it to Cosette. Valjean expertly scales the steep wall at the end of the alley and then pulls Cosette up to him. They find a way down from the wall just as Javert and his men enter the dark alley.

Valjean and Cosette find themselves in a vast, dark garden. They hear music and drop thankfully to their knees in prayer. A man approaches them with a bell clanging softly against his leg. Surprised, Valjean offers the man one hundred francs to let them spend the night in his lodgings. By incredible coincidence, the man is Fauchelevent, whom Valjean rescued from underneath a carriage in Montreuil. Fauchelevent addresses Valjean as M. Madeleine and declines his one hundred francs, remembering that Valjean once saved his life and found him a job. Fauchelevent tells Valjean that he and Cosette are in the garden of the convent of Petit-Picpus. He offers them a place to stay for the night. Valjean accepts, and they quickly move Cosette inside, out of the cold.

Book Five concludes with an explanation of how Javert manages to track down Valjean. Like the rest of the world, Javert thinks that Valjean died after his fall from the *Orion,* but the news of Cosette's kidnapping from the Thénardiers arouses his interest. The Thénardiers, anxious to hide their own crimes, say Cosette was retrieved by her grandfather. Their answer initially puts Javert's mind at ease, but when he hears the anecdotes about a "beggar who gives alms," he becomes suspicious again. After a brief investigation, Javert realizes that this man is really Valjean. He lies in wait on the night that Valjean flees the Gorbeau House, but he is so thrilled by the idea of hunting down Valjean that he intentionally toys with him and gives him time to get away. After carefully searching the area, Javert returns to police headquarters frustrated and ashamed.

ANALYSIS: BOOKS FOUR–FIVE

Valjean and Cosette's escape from the Gorbeau House begins a pattern of relocation and flight that continues throughout the novel, revealing how French society can make it difficult to find a home. Valjean and Cosette's constant movement reflects the advantages and pitfalls of the fluid social structure of the nineteenth-century city; while it is easy for them to disappear, it is difficult for them to settle down. Their neighbors are always strangers, which means that they can easily hide their troubled pasts, but it also means that these neighbors cannot be counted on for friendship and help when the truth about Valjean and his past comes out. Nor can Valjean or Cosette turn to their family for help, since the structure of poor families in nineteenth-century France is so loose and casual that neither of them knows where his or her surviving family members are. In a city that guarantees anonymity, Valjean and Cosette can depend only on each other. This is one of Hugo's sharpest criticisms of Parisian society, an environment whose families are dissolved and neighbors are only friendly if they are spies for the police.

Valjean and Cosette's flight from the Gorbeau House is motivated partly by Valjean's concern for Cosette. Although he has made many escape attempts before, this is the first time his flight is motivated by something greater than his simple instinct for self-preservation. Valjean recognizes that if he is caught, Cosette will most likely spend the rest of her childhood in the same kind of orphanages in which Fantine grew up and will lose any opportunity to improve her circumstances. Cosette's presence therefore adds a degree of legitimacy and urgency to Valjean's escape. We have already come to appreciate Valjean as a person, but now that his fate is tied up with Cosette's, we become even more concerned that his escape be successful.

The reappearance of Fauchelevent in the convent garden emphasizes the positive effects of good deeds. Fauchelevent's sudden appearance is so implausibly convenient, but Hugo is willing to sacrifice realism to show that good things happen to good people in times of need. Valjean's kindness thus far has brought him only trouble—his rescue of Fauchelevent raises Javert's initial suspicions, and the money Valjean gives the poor starts so much gossip that it leads Javert back to his trail. Now, however, Valjean's courageous rescue of Fauchelevent pays off when Valjean most needs help. With these turns of fate, Hugo encourages us to recognize the worth of helping others, even when doing so seems more trouble than it is worth. In return, Hugo suggests, we can expect the help of others during our own personal crises.

In Book Five, Javert's determination to recapture Valjean has become obsessive and maniacal, and his quest appears cruel and absurd. We see that even Javert is aware of the obsessive nature of his preoccupation with Valjean, since he keeps his suspicions to himself for fear that his colleagues will think him mad. Javert's manic determination to hunt down Valjean contradicts his claim that he is trying merely to uphold the law. His obsession with Valjean has clearly become a personal vendetta. Javert has always seen Valjean's prosperity as an affront to society and now sees Valjean's ability to escape from seemingly impossible situations as an affront to his own skills as a police officer. On a symbolic level, Valjean's ability to evade the police suggests that some higher force does not want Javert to capture Valjean—a notion that infuriates the uncompromising and logical Javert.

The inhumanity of Javert's persecution of Valjean is underscored by his lack of concern for Cosette. When Javert hears that an old man has kidnapped a girl from Montfermeil, he pursues the case not to ensure the girl's welfare but merely to track down his nemesis. Javert does not even inquire about the wretched conditions that Cosette endured under the Thénardiers. We sense that, given the chance, he would probably return the girl to their care. Javert's narrow-minded investigation into Cosette's alleged kidnapping further undermines his claim that he only wishes to uphold the law. By this point, it is apparent that Javert's only motive is to punish Valjean to the full extent of the law.

"COSETTE," BOOKS SIX–EIGHT

SUMMARY: BOOK SIX: PETIT-PICPUS

The narrator gives a brief history of the Petit-Picpus convent. The nuns are an order founded by the Spaniard Martin Verga, and their rituals are particularly severe. At any point in the day at least one nun is required to pray for the sins of the world while another kneels in devotion before the Holy Sacrament. The only men allowed inside the convent are the archbishop of the diocese and the gardener, who wears a bell on his leg to warn the nuns he is approaching. The nuns also run a boarding school. The girls at the school live in austerity, but they still manage to fill the school with signs of life. By 1840, the hard life at Petit-Picpus begins to take its toll. There are no new recruits, and the older nuns begin to die off.

SUMMARY: BOOK SEVEN: A PARENTHESIS

The narrator lauds the value of prayer and affirms that the principles of democracy and the spiritual benefits of religion do not necessarily contradict each other. At the same time, however, the narrator delivers a sharp criticism of monasticism—the practice of organizing secluded religious sects such as a convent or a monastery. Monasticism, the narrator claims, leads only to social isolation and religious fanaticism. The girls isolated within the convent do not have sufficient opportunities to learn about the world beyond the walls of Petit-Picpus. In effect, the convent is a religious prison.

SUMMARY: BOOK EIGHT:
CEMETERIES TAKE WHAT IS GIVEN THEM

With Fauchelevent's help, Valjean manages to seclude himself inside the convent of Petit-Picpus. Fauchelevent believes that Valjean, whom he continues to call M. Madeleine, has lost his fortune and is hiding from creditors. Fauchelevent offers to help Valjean find work as the convent's associate gardener. Valjean must first leave and reenter the convent, however, since the nuns will immediately suspect a strange man who appears out of nowhere.

Meanwhile, one of the nuns of the convent becomes ill and dies. The nuns wish to bury her in the convent, but Parisian law requires that she be buried in a municipal cemetery. The nuns persuade Fauchelevent to fill an empty coffin with dirt and deliver it to the cemetery in place of the nun's body. Fauchelevent is not convinced that the ruse will work. When Valjean hears of the dilemma, he suggests that Fauchelevent smuggle him out of the convent in the coffin. Despite some minor setbacks, the plan succeeds. Fauchelevent takes the coffin to the cemetery and is able to retrieve Valjean from the coffin by tricking the gravedigger. They return to the convent, where Fauchelevent tells the nuns that Valjean is his brother Ultimus. The convent hires Valjean and permits Cosette to enroll at the convent school. Valjean discovers that he is a natural gardener, and he and Cosette remain hidden and happy for some time.

ANALYSIS: BOOKS SIX–EIGHT

Valjean's near-burial in the coffin is a metaphor for the burial of his criminal past and assumption of a new identity. For the third time in the novel, Valjean resolves his problems by assuming a new identity, which means that his old persona must die for his new one to begin. We have seen this resurrection before, when Valjean falls off the *Orion* and fakes drowning before resurfacing in Montfermeil. Here, a literal coffin is used to emphasize the idea that the adoption of a new identity requires the death of the old one. Each time Valjean seemingly dies and assumes a new identity, however, he does more than simply repeat the same process. Each new identity puts more distance between Valjean and his criminal past. In his first reincarnation, Valjean discovers philanthropy and becomes Madeleine. When he rescues Cosette, he discovers love and takes on yet another identity. Now that Valjean has found genuine peace and seclusion, he sheds his previous identity and is reincarnated as a truly happy gardener and father figure.

Hugo's account of convent life highlights his religious philosophy, which embraces Christianity and its values but rejects the rigid dogma of the Church and its institutions. Hugo's simultaneous praise of Christianity and disdain for the Church is very much in keeping with the beliefs of many contemporary philosophers of the latter half of the nineteenth century, who thought that the Church distorted the original intent of Christian faith through corrupt, self-serving practices. Although Hugo largely avoids explicit criticism of the Church in *Les Misérables,* he does occasionally point to the corrupting influence of certain religious institutions. In Book Seven, for example, he suggests that the religious isolation of convents leads to zealotry and personal imbalance rather than any deeper understanding of God. Nonetheless, Hugo respects the convent's inflexibility more than the secular world's rigid laws. The convent's exemption from the laws governing the rest of French society provides Valjean with shelter and with the chance for rebirth.

Although the convent provides safe harbor for Valjean and Cosette, Hugo's negative views of the place imply that Cosette's entrance into the boarding school is a mixed blessing. The boarding school has its idyllic aspects, and it will provide Cosette with the kind of education that Hugo frequently champions. However, it is also a sort of rustic prison. It gives Cosette the opportunity to develop her intellect, but it forces her to do so within a secluded life that prevents her from developing her emotional and social intelligence. This lack of social interaction, particularly with boys, becomes more of a problem as Cosette approaches adolescence. This situation is optimal for Valjean, since he does not have to worry about Javert and since he has his beloved Cosette all to himself. The confinement of convent life, however, sows the seeds of a conflict that ultimately threatens to drive Cosette away from Valjean.

"MARIUS," BOOKS ONE–THREE

SUMMARY: BOOK ONE: PARIS ATOMIZED

On the streets of Paris lives a young street urchin named Gavroche. He is one of several hundred homeless children who roam the city, living in abandoned lots and underneath bridges. Gavroche's parents are none other than the Thénardiers—he is the unwanted third child whom we see as an infant in Montfermeil. The Thénardiers now live in the Gorbeau House under the pseudonym Jondrette. Cast out by his parents, Gavroche fends for himself on the street, begging and picking pockets to survive. He is only eleven or twelve years old, but he does not blame his parents for their neglect, since he has no idea how parents are supposed to behave.

SUMMARY: BOOK TWO: THE GRAND BOURGEOIS

The novel focuses on the life of Marius Pontmercy. Marius is a young man who has grown up under the care of his ninety-year-old maternal grandfather, Monsieur Gillenormand, a staunch supporter of the monarchy. Marius's father is Georges Pontmercy, a colonel in Napoléon's army. Pontmercy, persecuted for his support of Napoléon and plagued by Gillenormand's threats to disinherit Marius, eventually gives custody of Marius to his father-in-law.

SUMMARY: BOOK THREE:
THE GRANDFATHER AND THE GRANDSON

Marius does not hold much affection for his father, because Gillenormand has told him that his father abandoned him. In 1827, shortly after Marius turns eighteen, Gillenormand tells him that Marius's father is ill and orders him to visit his father. Marius rides out to Vernon, his father's hometown, the following morning but arrives a few minutes after his father dies. Since Marius has always believed that his father did not love him, he finds it difficult to grieve. Marius discovers a note among Pontmercy's belongings asking

Marius to find a man named Thénardier, who once saved Pont-mercy's life at Waterloo. The note instructs Marius to help Thénardier in any way he can.

Back in Paris, Marius struggles to understand his father's legacy. He wonders why his father, who supposedly did not love him, asked to see him before he died. The churchwarden, Mabeuf, tells Marius that his father came to Paris every two or three months to watch his son at Mass. This knowledge further confuses Marius. He immediately returns to Vernon to learn everything he can.

Marius devours history books and bulletins about his father's exploits in Napoléon's army and comes to admire the dead Pont-mercy. To the chagrin of his grandfather, Marius also becomes a passionate follower of Napoléon. Gillenormand learns of Marius's new political views, and the two get into a heated argument. Marius moves out, refusing any help or money from his family.

Analysis: Books One–Three

The different politics of the Gillenormand and Pontmercy house-holds represent the political trends dividing France in Hugo's time. Gillenormand, Pontmercy, and Marius each symbolize the major political trends of their respective generations. Gillenormand, the eldest of the three men, is a staunch supporter of the kings who ruled France in the centuries prior to the French Revolution of 1789. Pontmercy, on the other hand, is an ardent follower of Napoléon, who inherited the legacy of the 1789 revolution and acted as emperor of France until his defeat at Waterloo in 1815. After 1815, the royal family, the Bourbons, returned to power. To ensure that belief in the Napoléonic tradition is not passed down from father to son, Gillenormand intentionally isolates Marius from Pontmercy, raising him to support the Bourbons and oppose Napoléon. When Marius discovers that his father secretly loved him, however, he becomes more receptive to his father's beliefs and begins to examine them without prejudice. As a result of his research, Marius radically changes his political beliefs, which ultimately creates a rift between him and his grandfather. The split between Marius and Gillenor-mand, along with Marius's embrace of Napoléon, symbolizes the younger generation's rediscovery of the Napoléonic values and the principles of democracy.

While the Thénardiers' values have remained much the same, their move to Paris is a comment on the uprooted and debased nature of the French middle class following the restoration of the monarchy. Since leaving their inn in Montfermeil, the Thénardiers have become much poorer, and their greedy misbehavior has degenerated into serious con artistry and fraud. The Thénardiers' debased status is largely due to their obsession with money. Despite—or perhaps because of—their singular pursuit of francs, the Thénardiers are now worse off than they were in Montfermeil, since all of them are now packed into a wretched one-room tenement. Regardless of the cause of their misfortunes, however, the Thénardiers are a warning of what happens when one social class loses so much so quickly. Early on, the Thénardiers are petty swindlers, but their increasing poverty has made them so desperate and selfish that they go so far as to throw their youngest son, Gavroche, out onto the streets.

Gavroche exemplifies Hugo's belief that material wealth is unnecessary for—and can even impede—true happiness. Although Gavroche is the Thénardier who possesses the least, he is the happiest and most generous of the lot. He is less driven by the need for wealth and possessions, which makes him freer than the other Thénardiers to pursue his more authentic desires. Gavroche's carefree existence stands in striking contrast to the Thénardiers' home life, which consists of sitting idly in a cold, dark room all day, waiting for money from one of their schemes to come in. The difference between Gavroche and the rest of his family shows the misery that can accompany an obsession with money, as opposed to the happiness that can come with freedom.

"MARIUS," BOOKS FOUR–SEVEN

SUMMARY: BOOK FOUR: THE FRIENDS OF THE ABC

Marius meets a group of fellow law students who, like him, are becoming increasingly involved in politics at the expense of their studies. One of these students, Courfeyrac, becomes Marius's neighbor and introduces him to a secret political society called the Friends of the ABC. Led by the fiery Enjolras, the group believes ardently in social change. Marius thinks he has found an outlet for his political frustrations. One day, however, he argues with the other members of the group over Napoléon. Marius defends Napoléon and calls his empire a glorious episode in French history, while the other members are more interested in absolute democratic freedom.

Summary: Book Five:
The Excellence of Misfortune

Disappointed by the Friends of the ABC, Marius quits the group and begins to live on his own. He passes his law exams with flying colors but continues to live in utter poverty. He saves money however he can, but he often finds it is not enough. Marius's grandfather misses him and his aunt often tries to send him money, but he refuses to accept his family's support. The narrator concludes that poverty has been a blessing in disguise for Marius: freed from social obligations, he has been able to see what kind of man he really is. He becomes friends with the churchwarden, Mabeuf, who helps him through difficult times by getting him a job at a bookstore.

Summary: Book Six: The Conjunction of Two Stars

Despite his poverty, Marius develops into an attractive young man who often turns women's heads as he walks down the street. He is indifferent to women, however, until the day he sees Cosette sitting next to the elderly Valjean on a park bench in the Luxembourg Gardens. Marius is inexplicably drawn to her and goes to the gardens every day to catch a glimpse of her. He does not know Cosette's name, so he calls her "Lanoire," a nickname (coined by Courfeyrac) which means "the black one," because of her dark clothes. Courfeyrac has dubbed her companion "Leblanc," ("the white one") because of Valjean's white hair.

After a six-month absence, Marius returns to the gardens to find that the girl has blossomed into a beautiful young woman. Marius instantly falls in love with her. He discovers a handkerchief with the letter "U" stitched into it, which he believes to be hers, and Marius renames her Ursula. He improves his wardrobe and begins to follow the couple around the gardens. Leblanc quickly figures out what is going on. The following day, he sits at a different bench to see if Marius will follow. When Marius follows, Leblanc gives him a cold stare. Marius cannot help himself and follows his love home one day, asking the caretaker of the building on what floor the girl and the old man live. About a week later, the couple moves out without leaving a forwarding address.

Summary: Book Seven: Patron-Minette

The narrator introduces the criminal underworld of Paris, with its four ringleaders, Montparnasse, Babet, Claquesous, and Gueulemer. Each of these shadowy figures has his own subversive talents, but they operate together, like one monstrous figure with four heads. As a group, they are collectively called "Patron-Minette." They control all of the crime in their district of Paris and specialize in ambushes. Whenever anyone in their area wants to plan a robbery, he presents his plan to Patron-Minette, and the four men refine and execute it.

———————————

ANALYSIS: BOOKS FOUR–SEVEN

Marius's change in political allegiance from the Bourbon monarchy to the Friends of the ABC signals his break from the identity that others have imposed on him. Although Marius does harbor a growing interest in politics, he quickly grows tired of the rhetoric of Enjolras and the other Friends of the ABC. He begins to realize that his interest in politics has less to do with his views about freedom than with his sense of debt to his father, Pontmercy. Nonetheless, Marius's brief affiliation with the Friends of the ABC is beneficial since the experience teaches him to articulate his own personal beliefs. Marius's rift with Gillenormand, his refusal to accept money from his family, and his sudden adulation of his father are all manifestations of his attempts to figure out who he is and what his beliefs are. In breaking away from Gillenormand, Marius takes his first steps toward independence, and the ideas he explores and then rejects with the Friends of the ABC further enhance his self-understanding.

Marius pursues Cosette with an innocence that is touching to us but threatening to Valjean. The narrator tells us that Marius is not well-versed in love and intrigue. Indeed, Valjean's tests of Marius's interest in Cosette show that Marius is in fact a novice at love and flirtation. Whereas a more experienced man might try to mask his intent or directly approach the object of his desires, Marius is content to follow Cosette around the park innocently. Marius's charm lies in this very innocence, and the purity of his intentions, oddly enough, represents perhaps the greatest threat to Valjean. After all, it would be much easier for Valjean to justify protecting Cosette from a money-driven or sex-hungry prowler than from someone so completely and genuinely in love as Marius.

Hugo appeals to a wider readership by including scenes from the dangerous yet alluring Parisian criminal underworld. These scenes allow us to compare Valjean to real criminals. The emergence of complex crime rings was a popular topic in mid-nineteenth-century Paris and inspired the imagination of many authors of the time. Hugo describes the members of Patron-Minette in a tabloid fashion that is meant to mimic the sensationalist journalism of the time, which thrived on relating the darker side of Parisian life. Significantly, all the members of the criminal underworld change identities with ease, which reminds us that despite our warm feelings for Valjean, he is still considered a criminal. Although Valjean is certainly not immoral like Thénardier and his cronies, he also has a criminal background that emerged from poverty. The skills they have in common remind us that Valjean is, early in the novel, not so different from the men who soon try to rob him.

"MARIUS," BOOK EIGHT: THE NOXIOUS POOR

SUMMARY

> *[S]he wrote on a sheet of blank paper . . . "The cops are here."*
>
> (See QUOTATIONS, p. 67)

Marius spends several months trying to track down Cosette, whom he only knows as his beloved Ursula, the young woman from the Luxembourg Gardens, but she has disappeared, and he has grown despondent. Marius cannot stop thinking of her until a visit from his neighbor, Eponine Jondrette, reminds him that other people's troubles are worse than his own. Eponine comes to Marius's room in the Gorbeau House to ask for money. She is so emaciated that she has the body of girl but the broken voice of an old man. To show off the fact that she is literate, Eponine writes "The cops are here" on a piece of paper. Marius fails to realize that Eponine is attracted to him and offers her his last five francs.

Marius decides to take a more active interest in the welfare of the Jondrettes. He finds a crack in the wall that separates their apartments and is horrified by the sight of the squalor and poverty in which they live. Through the crack, Marius sees Eponine enter with a philanthropist and a young girl. He immediately recognizes the philanthropist as Leblanc and the girl as Ursula. Jondrette pretends to be an unemployed actor and begs Leblanc for rent money. Though the amount Jondrette is asking for is much higher than the rent, Leblanc vows to return later that evening to give him the money.

Marius overhears Jondrette plotting to rob and kill Leblanc when he returns that evening. Clearly, Jondrette and his wife recognize both Leblanc and Ursula from some past incident, and they seem infuriated to see their old acquaintances so well off. With the help of Patron-Minette, the local mob, the Jondrettes form a plan to coerce Leblanc into giving them a large sum of money. Although Marius does not fully understand the connection between the Jondrettes and Leblanc, he runs to the local police station. He tells an inspector about Jondrette's plan. The inspector, who turns out to be Javert, gives Marius two pistols and tells him to return to the Gorbeau House. Javert tells Marius that when the robbery has reached its peak, he should fire one of the pistols to signal to the police to enter the building and arrest the thieves.

Marius returns to his apartment. When Leblanc returns to the Gorbeau House, Jondrette and a number of local hoods—among them the members of Patron-Minette—ambush him. Leblanc calmly refuses to sign over any of his money, saying that he has none. Jondrette angrily reveals that his real name is Thénardier. Leblanc denies that he has ever met Thénardier before. Marius, recognizing the name Thénardier from his father's note, is faced with the dilemma of whether to help Leblanc or to protect the man who saved his father's life.

The Thénardiers force Valjean to write a note summoning Cosette to the apartment. Thénardier's messengers return with the news that Valjean has given them a false name and address. Thénardier is on the verge of killing Valjean when Marius sends Eponine's scribbled message—"The cops are here"—flying through the window. When the criminals read that the police have arrived, they try to flee, but Javert makes his entrance and arrests them all. In the confusion, Valjean slips out the window.

ANALYSIS

Thénardier's attempt to rob Leblanc is the climax of the "Marius" section of the novel, and it pulls together all the loose threads and unexplained coincidences that have occurred in the previous chapters. The episode shows Hugo's remarkable ability to use the smallest details from the past to make the most far-fetched parts of his story plausible. The incident is based on an extraordinary series of coincidences: Both Marius and the Thénardiers move into the same building where Valjean once lived; Thénardier happens to ask for money from Valjean, who is the father of Marius's beloved; the inspector for the precinct happens to be Javert; and Thénardier turns out to be the man who Marius's father thought saved his life at Waterloo. Although the overlap of so many different story lines is improbable, it is not inconceivable. For example, it makes sense that Marius and Thénardier might be neighbors, since Thénardier would appreciate the anonymity of the Gorbeau House and Marius would appreciate its low rent. Similarly, it is not surprising that the dogged Javert is still working in the last precinct where he knows Valjean lived. Lesser details also have a plausible explanation. Eponine has likely scribbled many warning notes in her criminal career, so writing "The cops are here" to prove her literacy is a logical choice for her. Thus, though the episode involves an unlikely combination of coincidences, Hugo roots the robbery so thoroughly in his earlier chapters that we can believe it.

The robbery scene forces Marius to choose between his different allegiances. While the climax does not resolve all of these conflicts, it does give us insight into Marius's character, especially his ability to find a middle ground. Marius does not, for instance, fire the pistol at the appointed moment since he does not want to betray his father's dying wish that he assist Thénardier in any way possible, but he does throw Eponine's letter into the Thénardiers' apartment. This split-second decision indicates Marius's newfound ability to balance his various allegiances while staying true to his own beliefs. While Marius does not betray Thénardier, he does prevent him from harming Valjean, whom Marius wishes to protect due to his love for Cosette. While Valjean and Javert are unyielding in their principles, Marius is more flexible and comes up with a way of thinking that is distinctly his own.

The Thénardiers' intricate schemes against Valjean show how thoroughly jealousy drives their criminal behavior. Unable to feel love and compassion themselves, the Thénardiers retaliate by plotting against those who are capable of such emotions. Mme. Thénardier's enraged reaction upon seeing that Cosette is better clothed than her own daughters represents her materialistic interpretation of the fact that Cosette is purer and more righteous than her children. Rather than try to learn how to become upstanding citizens themselves, the Thénardiers view respectability as an affront and try to drag Valjean and Cosette down to their own debased level of existence. The only members of the Thénardiers who do not suffer from these jealous urges are Gavroche, who no longer lives in the Thénardier household, and Eponine. Eponine's visit to Marius at the beginning of Book Eight foreshadows the selflessness she displays later in the novel.

"SAINT-DENIS," BOOKS ONE–SEVEN

SUMMARY: BOOK ONE: A FEW PAGES OF HISTORY

The narrator explains the causes and consequences of the 1830 July Revolution in France. After Napoléon's defeat at Waterloo in 1815, the monarchy tries to reassert the rights that it enjoyed before the French Revolution of 1789. Since the post-1815 government has been hampered by unsuccessful military campaigns and social injustice, the monarchy mistakenly believes that it can slowly rescind the rights it granted in 1815. When it attempts to do so, the government collapses, resulting in the July Revolution of 1830.

The new government, however, faces as many problems as the old one. The new king, Louis-Philippe, tries to find a middle ground among the different political factions but succeeds only in alienating all sides. His miscalculations lead to another revolution in 1832. Led by Enjolras, student revolutionaries begin to organize a massive political insurrection in the Faubourg Saint-Antoine, a district of Paris.

SUMMARY: BOOK TWO: EPONINE

Marius continues to obsess over Cosette. He still does not know her real name and refers to her as "the lark." He finds a park called the Field of the Lark and goes there every day to soothe the pain of his loss. Little does he know that Eponine, out of her love for Marius, has tracked down Cosette. Eponine tells Marius that Cosette and Valjean are living in Saint-Germain, a Paris suburb. Eponine does not tell Marius that she saw Cosette in the garden of the house while observing the house on behalf of an imprisoned robber. Eponine tells Marius to follow her to the house. He fails to realize that Eponine is in love with him and tries to hand her a five-franc coin. She sadly lets the coin fall to the ground and tells Marius that she does not want his money.

SUMMARY: BOOK THREE:
THE HOUSE ON THE RUE PLUMET

Tucked away in their house on Rue Plumet in Saint-Germain, Cosette and Valjean once again live a happy life free of fear. Nevertheless, problems begin to develop—not from outside this time, but from within. Cosette, who has lived with Valjean since she was eight years old, is blossoming into a young woman. She begins to sense that Valjean has chosen the seclusion of Saint-Germain for reasons other than merely hiding from Javert. Ever since Valjean ended their regular visits to the Luxembourg Gardens, it has become clear that he wants to hide Cosette from other men. Cosette thinks wistfully of the young man in the gardens. Having never had romance in his life, Valjean has no personal experience with love to help him relate to Cosette's yearnings for a man she has never met. At the same time, Valjean is painfully aware that Cosette is all that he has in life. Losing Cosette would mean losing everything.

SUMMARY: BOOK FOUR:
AID FROM BELOW OR FROM ABOVE

The street urchin Gavroche overhears Father Mabeuf worrying about his finances. Gavroche slips away and sees the murderous Montparnasse pounce on an old man. With great agility and strength, the old man, whom we recognize as Valjean, defends himself. He pins Montparnasse to the ground and lectures him about his life of crime. He then gives Montparnasse his wallet and lets Montparnasse go. Gavroche deftly picks Montparnasse's pocket and throws the wallet full of money over Mabeuf's wall. Mabeuf is ecstatic to find a wallet next to him, and his housekeeper declares that the money must have come from heaven.

SUMMARY: BOOK FIVE: AN END UNLIKE THE BEGINNING

After a few months of discord, Cosette and Valjean begin to live in harmony again. Their relationship reverts to the bliss they enjoyed during Cosette's childhood. Marius, however, interrupts this harmony. He has been spying on Cosette ever since Eponine gave him the address of the house in Saint-Germain. One night, he leaves a declaration of his love for Cosette. The next evening, after Valjean has left for his nightly walk around town, Marius enters the garden and professes his love for Cosette. She reciprocates Marius's feelings.

SUMMARY: BOOK SIX: LITTLE GAVROCHE

Back on the streets of Paris, Gavroche continues to practice his unique brand of street-smart philanthropy. He discovers two hungry, abandoned children and uses the little money he has to buy food for them, not realizing that they are his own younger brothers. Gavroche then runs into a woman who is freezing in the bitter cold and gives her enough of his own clothing to survive the night. Gavroche brings the two young boys to his makeshift home inside a giant statue of an elephant near the Bastille prison. Later that night, a number of criminals escape from prison, including his father, Thénardier. Gavroche rescues Thénardier from a rooftop, but his greedy father does not realize that his own son is the one helping him to escape.

SUMMARY: BOOK SEVEN: ARGOT

The narrator devotes several pages to an exploration of the rich vocabulary and origins of Parisian street slang.

ANALYSIS: BOOKS ONE–SEVEN

Like the convent before it, Valjean and Cosette's house in Saint-Germain is a sort of idyllic prison, a tranquil setting that creates tension between Cosette and Valjean. While Cosette no longer has to endure the severe discipline of the nuns, she no longer has any classmates to talk to and has only Valjean and the maid to keep her company. Valjean, on the other hand, appears to think all is well. Delighted to have Cosette all to himself and rid of the threat posed by Marius, he does not realize that his efforts to hold on to Cosette only make her more reluctant to stay with him. If anything, the isolated location of Saint-Germain leaves Cosette with more time to pine over Marius and realize her loneliness.

While Marius's naïveté is sometimes charming, it also blinds him to Eponine's feelings and makes him unwittingly insensitive and selfish. At times, his preoccupation with Cosette borders on addiction, resembling Javert's obsessive pursuit of Valjean more than courtship. Marius is so focused on his love for Cosette that he ignores Eponine, and he goes so far as to recruit her as a kind of carrier pigeon between him and his true love. Without knowing it, Marius insults Eponine by trying to pay her for her services. Eponine's response to this abuse is tragic, but we do feel some sense of encouragement in seeing a Thénardier act with such selflessness.

Eponine's attempts to ensure Marius's happiness are both sad and noble, and they are clearly preferable to the cruel cynicism her family has taught her.

Hugo again critiques the French justice system by demonstrating the corruption of the Parisian prisons. He suggests that dangerous criminals such as the leaders of Patron-Minette can effectively move in and out of prison as they see fit, provided they have the right connections and enough money to bribe the prison guards. The ease with which the Parisian crime ring circumvents the justice system contrasts with the tragic circumstances of Valjean, whose petty theft brought him a life of hardship and fear. Harsh prison sentences such as Valjean's can be justified only if the law comes down even more harshly on murderers. Hugo shows us that such is not the case, however. He implies that in French society justice is a resource like any other and that anyone who is well connected can exploit it at the expense of the unfortunate.

"SAINT-DENIS," BOOKS EIGHT–FIFTEEN

SUMMARY: BOOK EIGHT:
ENCHANTMENTS AND DESOLATIONS

As spring blossoms, so does the love between Marius and Cosette. Their bliss is almost dreamlike, but Valjean shatters their happiness when he announces that he plans to take Cosette to England in a week's time. Valjean is quite sure that their house is being watched and has seen Thénardier loitering around the neighborhood. Just as Valjean suspects, Thénardier is indeed plotting revenge and robbery, but Eponine manages to delay her father's plans. Valjean's desire to leave Paris is clearly motivated by a fear of losing Cosette, but it also stems from his unease about the deteriorating political stability in France.

When Cosette tells Marius about Valjean's plan, he is heartbroken. He goes to see Gillenormand, and although they have not yet reconciled, Marius begs his grandfather to grant him permission to marry Cosette. As they talk, Marius and Gillenormand begin to repair their relationship, but Gillenormand then makes the unfortunate suggestion that Marius make Cosette his mistress rather than marry her. Marius explodes, screaming that his grandfather has insulted his future wife and storms out of the house.

SUMMARY: BOOK NINE: WHERE ARE THEY GOING?

Marius returns to the house in Saint-Germain to see Cosette. When she fails to appear at the appointed time, Marius realizes that Cosette and Valjean have moved. Heartbroken, he has no time to grieve, since a mysterious voice advises him to join his friends on the barricades.

SUMMARY: BOOK TEN: JUNE 5, 1832

Paris is in the throes of a cholera epidemic, and the climate is so unstable that the slightest spark threatens to set off an insurrection. The spark finally comes on June 5, 1832, during the funeral procession of General Lamarque, a popular defender of liberty and the people. Fearing that the public mourning might lead to violence, the monarchy dispatches troops throughout Paris to maintain control. When shots are fired on the Austerlitz Bridge, the city explodes and barricades begin to spring up.

SUMMARY: BOOK ELEVEN:
THE ATOM FRATERNIZES WITH THE HURRICANE

Marius's former law-school companions, the Friends of the ABC, are among the first to answer the cries of revolution. The group begins to arm and prepare for the imminent confrontation with the army. Gavroche joins their ranks. As the mob marches through the streets, the old churchwarden Mabeuf joins them, following them doggedly even after they tell him to go home.

SUMMARY: BOOK TWELVE: CORINTH

The students decide to build a barricade around one of their favorite meeting spots, the Corinth wine-shop. Gavroche is instrumental in building the barricade and organizing its defense. The revolutionaries build barricades from everyday items, and they are in high spirits as night falls. Gavroche tries in vain to persuade the men to give him a gun. When the construction of the barricades is done, the men sit and wait. Gavroche suddenly realizes that an unnamed man who has joined the group is actually Javert, who is spying on them for the army. The men take Javert prisoner. One drunken revolutionary shoots a local homeowner, and Enjolras executes the man on the spot. Enjolras delivers a rousing speech. Marius's roommate, Courfeyrac, notices that a slim, young laborer who came looking for Marius earlier in the day has joined the group at the barricades.

SUMMARY: BOOK THIRTEEN: MARIUS ENTERS THE SHADOW
Mad with grief and eager to die, Marius takes the two pistols that Javert gives him earlier and heads toward the center of Paris. He walks toward the barricades like a man already dead.

SUMMARY: BOOK FOURTEEN: THE GRANDEUR OF DESPAIR
The government troops arrive and shoot down the revolutionary flag. Mabeuf climbs over the barricade to raise the flag once again, but the army shoots him dead. The students condemn Javert to death, but they keep him alive in the hopes of exchanging him for a revolutionary that the army is holding hostage. When they hear this revolutionary being executed, Enjolras decides that they will execute Javert ten minutes before the barricade falls. The soldiers attack the barricade and Marius shows up just in time to save Courfeyrac and Gavroche. Marius drives away the troops by threatening to blow up the barricade.

The fighting quickly becomes chaotic and Marius just barely avoids being killed. The mysterious young laborer, who is Eponine in disguise, saves Marius's life by throwing herself in front of a soldier's rifle. Eponine crawls toward Marius and confesses her love to him. She hands Marius a letter from Cosette and dies. After kissing Eponine's lifeless face, Marius reads the letter, in which Cosette reveals her whereabouts. Marius writes Cosette a letter telling her he will die on the barricades and bidding her farewell. Marius sends Gavroche to deliver the news.

SUMMARY: BOOK FIFTEEN: THE RUE DE L'HOMME-ARMÉ
Gavroche runs through the streets with Marius's letter. Valjean intercepts the boy and says that he will deliver the letter to Cosette himself. Gavroche is scornful at first, then feels sympathy for the old man and gives him the letter. Valjean asks Gavroche where the barricade is. The boy answers and runs off into the night. When Valjean reads the letter, he at first rejoices that Marius will soon cease to be a threat to his happiness. Valjean's decency soon takes over, however, and, dressed as a member of the National Guard, he heads toward the barricade.

ANALYSIS: BOOKS EIGHT–FIFTEEN
Though she is a Thénardier and has a criminal record, Eponine emerges in this section as one of the most virtuous figures in the

novel. Her love for Marius leads her to serve as a messenger between Marius and her rival, Cosette, and she takes this thankless task further when she helps protect Cosette. Eponine tries to divert Patron-Minette's attention away from Valjean's house, putting her own safety at risk when she threatens to wake up the whole neighborhood if Thénardier and his cronies break into the house. Likewise, Eponine urges Valjean to move away when she becomes aware that her father is planning another attack. Ultimately, her love for Marius results in her death when she throws herself in front of a rifle to save him. Eponine, who grows up in the unloving environment of the Thénardier household, is a tragic figure. The fact that the daughter of a couple as despicable as the Thénardiers is capable of such love and selflessness implies that anyone—regardless of his or her upbringing or social status—can rise above terrible circumstances and become virtuous.

Marius's failed reconciliation with his grandfather highlights the social prejudices that Hugo sought to combat by writing *Les Misérables*. Upon hearing that Marius wants to marry a girl who possesses neither a dowry nor any apparent income, Gillenormand suggests that an affair might be more appropriate than marriage. In his mind, lower-class women have nothing to offer other than their bodies, and he advises Marius accordingly. Though offensive, Gillenormand's suggestion might seem harmless if it were not for the fact that it reminds us of Tholomyès's behavior. Tholomyès, Cosette's father, is an upper-class student who holds the same cavalier views toward lower-class women as Gillenormand does, and his behavior has disastrous effects for the women with whom he is involved. Tholomyès's affair with Fantine, for example, starts her on the road to prostitution and incarceration. Marius's horrified response to his grandfather's suggestion distinguishes Marius as a man of honor and gives us some faith in the morals of upper-class students. Gillenormand's proposal reveals the callous attitude of the upper class toward the working poor and shows us that Tholomyès's behavior would have been applauded and condoned by the other men in his upper-class world.

While Hugo's sympathies lie with the revolutionaries, he is too disgusted with bloodshed to portray the insurrection as a glorious moment in French history. He shows us small acts of heroism, such as Mabeuf's attempt to rescue the flag, but he primarily portrays the barricade as a place of unnecessary brutality and pointless violence. Enjolras's execution of one of his own men for killing a civilian is justifiable, but it makes us wonder whether even the most princi-pled violence might inevitably lead to murder and mayhem of the worst kind. In contrast to the example Enjolras and his men set, Valjean avoids killing anyone, even his most bitter enemy. Hugo suggests that revolution does not have to involve violence and that the only truly revolutionary weapons are forgiveness and kindness.

"JEAN VALJEAN," BOOKS ONE–THREE

SUMMARY: BOOK ONE: WAR BETWEEN FOUR WALLS
The revolutionaries are temporarily victorious, but their morale falls when they learn that the rest of the city has failed to join their uprising. The army prepares another attack on the barricade, prompting Enjolras to urge all revolutionaries who have wives and children to return to their families. Though the men refuse, Enjolras insists, and the group votes on which five men to send away. Enjol-ras, however, has only enough army uniforms for four men to slip out in disguise. Out of nowhere, Valjean appears and offers to give up his own uniform for the fifth man.

Valjean is a valiant fighter but makes a point of not killing any of the enemy. Enjolras expresses regret at taking lives, but he is willing to kill for his beliefs. When the revolutionaries run low on ammuni-tion, Gavroche bravely scrambles over the barricade to gather ammunition from the bodies of dead army soldiers. He almost returns to the barricades unharmed, but at the last minute he is shot twice and dies. Realizing that the army is about to storm the barri-cade, Enjolras orders Javert's execution, and Valjean eagerly volun-teers. Once they are alone, however, Valjean tells Javert his address and sets him free. Valjean fires a shot in the air so the others will think that he has executed Javert. When he rejoins the group at the barricade, Marius looks at him with dread.

The revolutionaries can no longer stave off the attackers, so Enjolras orders a retreat. They fall back into the Corinth wine-shop. Marius is shot, but Valjean catches him as he falls and carries him off. When the troops enter the wine-shop, they find only Enjol-ras. He is executed as the army hunts down and kills the remaining revolutionaries. Valjean, with the unconscious Marius slung over his shoulders, searches for an escape. All exits are sealed and the troops are fast approaching. Luckily, Valjean discovers a sewer grate and carries Marius down into the sewers with him.

SUMMARY: BOOK TWO: THE INTESTINE OF LEVIATHAN
The narrator bemoans the fact that Paris spends huge sums collecting bird droppings for fertilizer while washing out all the human waste that could serve the same purpose. We learn that the Paris sewers were once nightmarish places and are told of the great flood in 1802, which covered large parts of the city with waste and filth. A man named Bruneseau began an extensive redesign of the sewers. The work was finished years later, after a cholera outbreak.

SUMMARY: BOOK THREE: MIRE, BUT SOUL
It is clear that Marius desperately needs a doctor. Valjean can barely see in the darkness of the filthy sewers, but his instincts guide him toward the river Seine, and he rushes ahead to bring Marius to safety. Avoiding police patrols and fighting fatigue and hunger, Valjean finally stumbles upon an exit. To his dismay, he finds that the gate is locked and cannot be forced open. Thénardier appears out of the darkness, demanding money in exchange for opening the gate. Thénardier does not recognize Valjean and assumes he is merely a criminal who has killed a wealthy man. Marius has no money, and Valjean is carrying only a paltry sum. Thénardier reluctantly takes the money and opens the gate. He also rips off a piece of Marius's jacket so that he can later identify Valjean's victim.

Valjean emerges on the banks of the Seine, but his freedom is short-lived. Javert, who has been chasing Thénardier, is waiting at the sewer entrance. Valjean is so covered in mud and slime that Javert does not recognize him, but Valjean turns himself in anyway. Valjean begs Javert to let him return Marius, who is dying, to his grandfather. Javert agrees and takes them to Gillenormand's house. After Valjean and Javert drop off the wounded Marius at Gillenormand's house, Valjean asks Javert for one more favor: he wants to see Cosette one last time. Again, Javert agrees to Valjean's request. Valjean goes up the stairs to see his adopted daughter with a heavy heart, but when he looks out the window, he is surprised to see that Javert is gone.

ANALYSIS: BOOKS ONE–THREE
Valjean's offer to execute Javert for the revolutionaries turns out to be a gesture of compassion and concern, and befuddles the hardhearted Javert. When Valjean brings Javert into the empty courtyard, Javert thinks that Valjean is finally going to punish him for his

years of obsessive pursuit. It turns out, however, that not only does Valjean have no intention of executing Javert, but he also goes out of his way to save his tormentor's life. By faking Javert's execution, Valjean ensures that no one else kills the inspector. Javert is floored by Valjean's inherent goodness, and his belief in his cause starts to waver. Unlike before, when Valjean has to beg Javert to let him retrieve Cosette in Montreuil, Javert now allows Valjean one favor, permitting him to bring Marius back to his grandfather's. Valjean acts the part of Javert's executioner almost too well, and there is an important moment of foreshadowing when Marius recoils from Valjean in horror. As far as Marius can tell, Valjean is a murderer, and as long as Marius remains unaware that Valjean has saved both his and Javert's lives, he does not change his opinion.

Valjean arrives at the barricade just in time to save one unnamed man from certain death, a moment strongly reminiscent of his salvation of Cosette in the woods outside the Thénardiers' inn. This episode at the barricade reinforces our perception of Valjean as a nearly providential figure who arrives when people need him most. Just as he seems to drop from the sky in answer to Cosette's desperate plea for help, Valjean once again appears out of nowhere to come to the rescue of one of the five men chosen to sneak out of the barricade. In describing Valjean's generosity, the narrator writes that "[a] fifth uniform dropped, as if from heaven, onto the four others." Phrased in these terms, Valjean's uniform is like the giant hand that helps the young Cosette with her pail of water, a vehicle sent from heaven to help the unfortunate. Valjean's criminal past, which has taught him to slip in and out of places unnoticed, contributes to his otherworldly air and turns him into a *deus ex machina*, a literary device in which a character or event unexpectedly swoops in to resolve a difficult situation. The *deus ex machina* is a device commonly used in drama, and Hugo's use of it here highlights the impact of his theatrical background on his novel. It also reveals Hugo's enormous faith in his protagonist: Valjean is so decent and good that the rules of the everyday world no longer apply to him. Indeed, his helpful appearances are worthy of an angel.

"JEAN VALJEAN," BOOKS FOUR–NINE

SUMMARY: BOOK FOUR: JAVERT OFF THE TRACK

> [T]o betray society in order to be true to his own
> conscience . . . this is what prostrated him.
> (See QUOTATIONS, p. 68)

After leaving Valjean at his house, Javert wanders the streets of Paris lost in thought. For the first time in his life, he is racked by indecision. He feels that turning in Valjean would be ignoble and undignified, but as an officer of the law he feels he cannot let his man go. Javert's only goal in life is to be beyond reproach, but Valjean's mercy makes it impossible for him to remain true to this goal. With a final note of resolution, Javert writes a letter to the prefect of the Parisian police with several suggestions about various matters of discipline and prison life. Javert then walks to the raging Seine, spends some time watching the waters flow by, and finally throws himself in and drowns.

SUMMARY: BOOK FIVE: GRANDSON AND GRANDFATHER

Marius makes a slow recovery in his grandfather's home, unaware that it is Valjean who rescued him from the barricades. Marius has suffered a broken collarbone and lost a lot of blood from his many wounds. After six months with a raging fever, he makes a full recovery, and his thoughts turn immediately to Cosette. Eager to reestablish good terms with his beloved grandson, Gillenormand grants Marius permission to marry Cosette. He does so with some reservation, since he still believes that Cosette is a simple working-class girl without any money. When Gillenormand finally meets Cosette, he is amazed by her beauty and shocked when Valjean tells him that Cosette will have a dowry of 600,000 francs. Cosette and Marius are not interested in such financial matters, and Marius declares his undying love for Cosette.

SUMMARY: BOOK SIX: THE WHITE NIGHT

Because Valjean is the only one who knows about Cosette's illegitimate birth, there are no more obstacles in the way of Cosette and Marius's marital bliss. A few days before the wedding, Valjean fakes an accident with his writing hand. The others do not realize that it is merely a ruse so that he will not have to forge a false name on the marriage certificate. The ruse works, and Gillenormand signs all the necessary documents instead. The wedding day is a happy one, and Cosette moves into the Gillenormand household. Valjean, however, spends the night lost in thought, distraught that he is losing the only person he has ever loved.

Summary: Book Seven: The Last Drop in the Chalice

Now that Cosette is married, Valjean feels compelled to confess his criminal past. He goes to Marius's house and tells the young man everything. Marius is shocked by Valjean's revelations and at first refuses to believe them. Valjean almost breaks down in his attempts to convince Marius that he is telling the truth. Marius finally accepts Valjean's statements as the truth and offers to arrange for a pardon, but Valjean refuses. Cosette, flushed with happiness, comes into the room and jokes with the two men, and she pouts playfully when they send her away. Marius agrees with Valjean that it would be best if Valjean never saw Cosette again. In the end, however, Valjean caves and asks that he be allowed to see Cosette in the evenings at least. Marius agrees. Once Valjean leaves, Marius begins to regard his father-in-law as a criminal, a belief that is cemented by the fact that Marius thinks Valjean really did execute Javert on the barricade. Marius also begins to doubt the legitimacy of Cosette's dowry.

Summary: Book Eight: The Twilight Wane

Unknown to Cosette, Marius slowly pushes Valjean out of her life. Marius ensures that Valjean's visits become less frequent, and when Valjean does come to the house he is received only in the unfurnished cellar below the parlor. Depressed at having lost Cosette forever, Valjean returns to his apartment. He takes to his bed and catches a fever. As he lies in his room in misery, Valjean thinks that he will never see Cosette again and that death cannot come soon enough.

Summary: Book Nine: Supreme Shadow, Supreme Dawn

Thénardier visits Marius a few weeks later, disguised as a statesman. He tells Marius that he has information about Valjean that he is willing to sell. Marius tells Thénardier his disguise is useless, since he knows who Thénardier really is, and contemptuously pays Thénardier five hundred francs. Thénardier reveals that Valjean earned Cosette's dowry legitimately from his work as a manufacturer under the name Madeleine. He also tells Marius that Javert was not murdered, but actually killed himself.

Marius wonders aloud that Valjean might actually be an honest man. Thénardier contradicts him, saying that Valjean is in fact a thief and a murderer. To prove it, he tells Marius of his encounter with Valjean and his victim in the sewer. He produces the piece of cloth that he tore from the victim's jacket as proof. Marius rushes to a closet and pulls out his bloodied jacket, and the fragment of fabric fits exactly. He throws money at Thénardier and orders him out of the house. The incorrigible Thénardier, we are told, uses the money to leave for America, where he becomes a slave-trader.

Marius realizes that Valjean is the man who saved him on the barricades and brought him home through the sewers. Overcome with guilt, Marius tells Cosette about his discovery. The couple rushes to Valjean's apartment to see him. They find him ill and bedridden, but he is overjoyed to see them. Overcome, Valjean embraces Cosette one last time and dies in happiness.

> [Valjean] had fallen back, the light from the candlesticks fell across him; his white face looked up toward heaven. . . .
>
> (See QUOTATIONS, p. 69)

ANALYSIS: BOOKS FOUR–NINE

Though Valjean's compassion helps persuade Javert to release him, what ultimately defeats Javert is not emotion but logic. Valjean's unconditional love for others weakens the stern Javert not because it moves him, but because it makes it impossible for him to justify his inflexible interpretation of the law. Suddenly, Javert and his dogged sense of duty no longer appear honorable and beyond reproach. In the end, Javert cannot bring himself to arrest Valjean because such an action would make no sense. Javert does not believe that Valjean is innocent, but he does believe that Valjean is good, and that to arrest him would debase the moral authority of the law. For the exceedingly practical Javert, therefore, the only way out of his dilemma is to remove himself from it altogether, and suicide becomes the next logical step. While his suicide is a powerful and poignant moment, Javert himself never becomes emotional. He dies in the same way he has lived: determined and resolute.

Hugo employs all of his descriptive talents as Javert prepares to make his final exit in Book Four of the novel's final section, and we see Hugo's descriptive style at work throughout this section. We see Javert "plung[ing]" into the streets—a word choice that foreshadows his imminent leap into the river. We also see him passing a number of Parisian locales that have played a prominent role in French history. Even when Javert is alone, Hugo manages to incorporate historical references and vivid urban descriptions. Hugo also infuses this section of *Les Misérables* with symbolism, especially in the scene in which Javert walks past the Grève, a place where public executions are staged. The mention of this particular site standing empty reveals the hollowness of Javert's adherence to the law and hints at the harsh judgment he will impose on himself.

Thénardier's final appearance in the novel resolves the story's last major conflict and raises questions about the nature of injustice everywhere. Thénardier intends to extort money from Marius and defame both Cosette and Valjean, but instead he ends up bringing about their reconciliation. We may question whether the ending is truly just, since Thénardier is never held accountable for his crimes while Valjean becomes ill and dies. From Hugo's perspective, however, both characters get the end they deserve. Thénardier, who has never felt real satisfaction and fulfillment, will continue to live in vain. Valjean, on the other hand, dies happy and content, and he is redeemed in the eyes of others. Thénardier's journey for America has a double meaning. On the one hand, the departure of one of Paris's worst criminals suggests that French society as a whole is being purged of liars and cheats. On the other hand, it allows Hugo to broaden his sights and suggest that injustice is a worldwide problem. By making Thénardier become a slave-trader, Hugo points to foreign injustices, such as slavery in America.

Valjean's final words indicate the fulfillment of the promise he makes to Myriel, the bishop of Digne, at the very beginning of the novel. In the spirit Myriel has instilled in him, Valjean preaches forgiveness, explaining that love is the most important thing that exists and that even people such as the Thénardiers must be forgiven. In the same way that Valjean's dying words recall his promise to Myriel, the physical setting of the room evokes his stay at Myriel's house in Digne. The description of Valjean's death reminds us of the description of the sleeping Myriel: "[T]he light from the candlesticks fell across [Valjean]; his white face looked up toward heaven." The candlesticks are the same ones that Myriel gives to Valjean so many years earlier, and the light they cast symbolizes Myriel's approval and recognition of a virtuous man's redemption.

SUMMARY & ANALYSIS

Important Quotations
Explained

1. [Valjean] strained his eyes in the distance and called
    out . . . "Petit Gervais! . . ." His cries died away into
    the mist, without even awaking an echo. . . . [H]is
    knees suddenly bent under him, as if an invisible
    power suddenly overwhelmed him with the weight of
    his bad conscience; he fell exhausted . . . and cried out,
    "I'm such a miserable man!"

Valjean's encounter with Petit Gervais in Book II of "Fantine" is the
first interaction Valjean has after he leaves Myriel's house in Digne.
Valjean's inability to keep his promise to become an honest man
makes him realize how immoral he has become. Hugo's language in
this passage emphasizes the gravity of this realization and portrays
Valjean as physically collapsing under the weight of his conscience.
The desolate setting in which Valjean's epiphany takes place reflects
the extent to which he has isolated himself from others. Valjean
receives no response when he pleads for forgiveness, not even his
own echo. The desolation also suggests that there is an emptiness in
Valjean's soul, which he does not realize until his encounter with
Myriel. This emptiness is expressed by Valjean when he calls himself
"miserable," a word that connotes both wretched behavior and
unhappiness. For the first time in nearly two decades, Valjean
acknowledges his transgressions. By doing so he is finally able to feel
compassion for his victim and recognize his own unhappiness. This
scene marks the crucial turning point in Valjean's life, in which he
begins to transform from a thief into a philanthropist.

2.   [T]he poor little despairing thing could not help
crying: "Oh my God! Oh God!"

At that moment she suddenly felt that the weight of
the bucket was gone. A hand, which seemed enormous
to her, had just caught the handle, and was carrying it
easily. . . .

. . .

The child was not afraid.

This passage occurs in Book III of "Cosette," after Mme. Thénardier
orders Cosette to fetch a pail of water from the forest. Hugo uses
especially melodramatic language and imagery to underscore the
nightmarish quality of Cosette's life with the Thénardiers and the
almost divine appearance of Valjean. In describing Cosette's despair,
Hugo foregoes realism in favor of prose that could have come from
a ghost story. The forest is dark and frightening, and it never seems
to end—a metaphor for Cosette's life as a near-slave at the inn in
Montfermeil. This haunted setting also sets the stage for Valjean's
entrance, since he first appears as a disembodied hand. However, the
fact that Cosette is not afraid and that the hand appears immediately
after she prays to God gives Valjean an unmistakably saintly quality.
He has acted as a decent man since his conversion at Digne, but now
he appears almost angelic. Hugo even gives Valjean a Christlike
aspect by setting this scene on Christmas Eve, an evening in Christian tradition that is part of the celebration of Jesus' birth. This scene
represents the beginning of Valjean and Cosette's life together and
affirms Valjean's role as Cosette's savior from the wicked
Thénardiers.

QUOTATIONS

3. "Here, I am going to write something to show you."
    . . . [S]he wrote on a sheet of blank paper . . . "The
    cops are here."

This snippet describes Eponine's excitement in Book VIII of "Marius" as she tries to impress Marius at the Gorbeau House. This incident gives us insight into the Thénardiers' circumstances and the importance that Hugo placed on education and literacy. It is significant that Eponine chooses to write the phrase "The cops are here" as proof that she is literate, since it shows that she considers this an ordinary catchphrase; clearly, law enforcement is a regular presence in the Thénardiers' lives. The great pride that Eponine takes in the fact that she can write emphasizes that most other women of Eponine's social standing cannot. Throughout the novel, Hugo places great importance on literacy—in a few instances, in fact, being able to read or write makes the difference between falling prey to and avoiding catastrophe. Earlier in the novel, we see illiteracy lead to Fantine's exposure and subsequent loss of her job. Now, Eponine's nonchalant scribbling thwarts Thénardier's ambush and saves Valjean. In both instances, Hugo turns the ability to write into more than just an educational asset, suggesting that, when we least expect it, writing can make the difference between life and death.

QUOTATIONS

4.   To owe life to a malefactor . . . to be, in spite of
      himself, on a level with a fugitive from justice . . . to
      betray society in order to be true to his own
      conscience; that all these absurdities . . . should
      accumulate on himself—this is what prostrated him.

This passage from Book IV of "Jean Valjean" describes Javert's state of mind before he commits suicide. We see the extent to which Valjean's mercy and compassion shatter Javert's way of life. Torn between his inflexible enforcement of the letter of the law and his personal debt to Valjean, Javert becomes profoundly confused. While Javert's response is not particularly emotional, Valjean's unconditional love for his fellow human completely disarms the stern Javert and makes it impossible for him to continue his duty with honor. Javert struggles to understand how a straightforward, literal interpretation of the law can be at odds with the spirit of the law. Seeing no alternative, he resolves his inner crisis by committing suicide.

It is important to note that Javert does not kill himself out of guilt or remorse, but because to be true to his conscience would be "to betray society"—an option that is equally unacceptable to Javert. Hugo's presentation of Javert's quandary exemplifies his tendency to blend the narrator's voice with the tone of the characters that he describes. The omniscient observer is always privy to the thoughts and motivations of the novel's characters, but here the narrator gets inside Javert's head and mimics his thought process. The close connection between Hugo's narrative voice and the minds of his characters is accomplished by Hugo's use of run-on sentences in this passage, which are written as if Javert's thoughts were unfolding in front of us.

QUOTATIONS

5.   [Valjean] had fallen back, the light from the
      candlesticks fell across him; his white face looked up
      toward heaven, he let Cosette and Marius cover his
      hands with kisses; he was dead.

This passage, from Book IX of "Jean Valjean" brings Valjean's personal journey full circle and compares him to his inspiration,
Myriel, the bishop of Digne. The light that falls on Valjean's face is
reminiscent of the scene early in the novel in which Valjean steals
Myriel's silver. There, we see the bishop's face surrounded by light as
he lies in the bed, just as we see light on Valjean's face here. The brilliant moonlight of the earlier scene symbolizes Myriel's goodness
and God's love of him. Here we infer that the same is true of Valjean.
The mention of the candlesticks is a reminder of Valjean's promise
to Myriel to become a better man. The candlesticks are the same
ones Myriel gives Valjean so many years earlier, and the light they
cast affirms that Valjean's criminal past has been redeemed by his
virtuous acts.

Valjean dies a happy death, knowing that he has become a loving, compassionate man. His transcendence stems from his ability
to care for other human beings—an ability we see when he refers to
Cosette and Marius as his "children" just before this passage. In
addition to highlighting Valjean's kindness, his use of the word
"children" also implies that his legacy of love and compassion has
been passed on to Marius and Cosette.

QUOTATIONS

KEY FACTS

FULL TITLE
Les Misérables

AUTHOR
Victor Hugo

TYPE OF WORK
Novel

GENRE
Epic novel; historical novel

LANGUAGE
French

TIME AND PLACE WRITTEN
1845–1862; Paris and the Channel Islands (English possessions off the coast of France)

DATE OF FIRST PUBLICATION
1862

PUBLISHER
Pagnerre (Paris)

NARRATOR
An anonymous narrator

POINT OF VIEW
The story is told from the perspective of an omniscient narrator who frequently addresses us. The narrator not only knows what the characters are thinking at all times but also has a detailed grasp of contemporary politics and society.

TONE
The tone tends to reflect the narrator's empathy with the characters. When describing broader trends in politics and society, the tone reflects Hugo's outspoken views on social reform.

TENSE
Past

SETTING (TIME)
  1789–1832

SETTING (PLACE)
  France; primarily the cities of Arras, Digne, Montreuil-sur-mer,
  Montfermeil, Paris, and Toulon

PROTAGONIST
  Jean Valjean

MAJOR CONFLICT
  Valjean struggles to transform himself from a thief into an
  honest man; over the years he struggles to stay a step ahead of
  the zealous police officer Javert and tries to raise his adopted
  daughter, Cosette.

RISING ACTION
  Valjean's disclosure of his true identity at Champmathieu's trial;
  Valjean's rescue of Cosette from the Thénardiers; Marius's first
  sight of Cosette in the Luxembourg Gardens.

CLIMAX
  Marius, Valjean, and Javert's dramatic interactions at
  the barricades

FALLING ACTION
  Marius and Cosette's wedding; Javert's suicide

THEMES
  The importance of love and compassion; social injustice in
  nineteenth-century France; the long-term effects of the French
  Revolution on French society

MOTIFS
  The plight of orphans; disguises and pseudonyms; resurrection

SYMBOLS
  Myriel's silver candlesticks; snakes, insects, and birds

FORESHADOWING
  The novel hints that Monsieur Madeleine is in fact Jean Valjean.

KEY FACTS

Study Questions & Essay Topics

Study Questions

1. *What are the factors leading to Fantine's decline?*

Fantine's misfortunes are rooted in her naïveté and a poor education, which in many ways stem from the social imbalances of nineteenth-century French society. Innocent to the ways of the world, Fantine falls in love with Tholomyès, a debonair upper-class student who obeys upper-class social customs and leaves Fantine even though she is pregnant with his child. She struggles to support herself and her child, and when Paris proves too much for her, she returns to Montreuil-sur-mer. Because her illegitimate child would certainly not make anyone want to hire her, she leaves her beloved Cosette with strangers. Even this move does not save Fantine, as she cannot read or write, and must resort to dictating her letters to Cosette to a gossipy scribe who promptly spreads the news. In the end, Fantine has no choice but to become a prostitute—a move that forces her further out into the fringes of society and eventually into the hands of the police. While there are certainly a number of factors that contribute to Fantine's decline, Hugo suggests that her poor schooling and boorish lover condemn her to a life of poverty before she even leaves Paris, and that the misfortunes that befall Fantine in Montreuil are the inevitable results of these two initial circumstances.

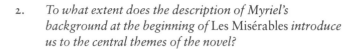

2. *To what extent does the description of Myriel's background at the beginning of* Les Misérables *introduce us to the central themes of the novel?*

The novel begins with a brief biography of Myriel. We learn that he was forced into exile during the French Revolution and rose quickly to become the bishop of Digne upon his return to France. From the outset of the novel, therefore, Hugo confronts us with the turbulent history of the time period in which the novel takes place. As bishop of Digne, Myriel strives to compensate for the vast inequalities between the rich and poor under his care. He even goes so far as to give up his own material comfort to improve the welfare of his parishioners. Myriel's selflessness thus serves as our introduction to the many social injustices in France, and highlights the power of love and compassion to overcome these injustices. Hugo establishes Myriel as a man of compassion, the yardstick against which Valjean measures his own success in becoming an honest man. By beginning his novel with the story of Myriel, Hugo hopes we will, like Valjean, understand that this kind of charity is what is needed in such turbulent times. Through Myriel, we understand what a decent man should be and the extent of what he can achieve.

3. *What are the central conflicts that lead Marius to leave
    Gillenormand's house? How does he resolve them?*

Marius leaves his grandfather's house in order to make sense of his
conflicting allegiances. Until the age of eighteen, Marius is led to
believe that his father, Georges Pontmercy, has abandoned him.
When Marius learns that his grandfather, Gillenormand, has intentionally kept him apart from his father, he rebels against his grandfather by becoming a staunch supporter of Napoléon Bonaparte
and storming out of the house. The issue at stake is largely political
but also represents a son's angry attempt to reconcile himself with
his dead father. Once he attains some distance from his family, Marius is able to investigate his father's life and makes a real connection
to his father when he participates in the insurrection of 1832. This
action is almost fatal, but when Marius recovers from his wounds,
he is finally ready to reconcile himself with his grandfather. Once
Marius finally understands and relives his father's legacy, he is
secure enough in himself that he can return to his old home. Marius
does not, in the end, choose his father over his grandfather. Instead,
he incorporates what he has learned from both of them into a personality that is distinctly his own.

SUGGESTED ESSAY TOPICS

1. Discuss the role that family allegiance plays in the lives of Cosette, Marius, and Gavroche.

2. How do you account for Eponine's selflessness? Is it significant that one of Hugo's most noble characters is a member of the Thénardier family?

3. Discuss Hugo's treatment of the Industrial Revolution. Is there any one place or city that best represents the pros and cons of industry?

4. What ultimately drives Javert to suicide?

5. How do Hugo's descriptions of Paris relate to the central themes of the novel?

6. Discuss the ways in which Valjean both helps and hinders Cosette as she becomes an adult.

QUESTIONS & ESSAYS

Review & Resources

Quiz

1. On the barricade, why does Eponine throw herself in front of the soldier's rifle?

   A. She decides that her beliefs are more important to her than her life
   B. She is in love with Marius
   C. She is suicidal
   D. She wants to make Cosette suffer

2. Who is not a blood member of the Thénardier family?

   A. Cosette
   B. Eponine
   C. Azelma
   D. Gavroche

3. Why does Myriel let Valjean spend the night in his house?

   A. He thinks that Valjean has money
   B. Because Valjean once saved Myriel's life
   C. He wants to treat his fellow man with kindness and respect
   D. He wants to convert Valjean to Christianity

4. Which of the following solves Montreuil-sur-mer's economic problems?

   A. Madeleine's manufacturing innovations
   B. The insurrection led by the Friends of the ABC
   C. Fantine's prostitution ring
   D. Javert's pyramid schemes

5. Why does Thénardier save Georges Pontmercy's life?

    A. Because the two men are lifelong friends
    B. He does so by accident
    C. He wants to find a suitable husband for Eponine
    D. He admires the general's contributions to the empire

6. Who is Cosette's biological father?

    A. Tholomyès
    B. Thénardier
    C. Montparnasse
    D. Valjean

7. Why does Fauchelevent let Valjean and Cosette stay in the convent?

    A. He is in love with Cosette
    B. He is Marius's grandfather
    C. Valjean once saved his life
    D. He is spying for Javert

8. What does Javert do near the end of the novel?

    A. He commits suicide
    B. He marries Cosette
    C. He becomes a beggar
    D. He fights in the insurrection

9. Where does Marius first see Cosette?

    A. The Gorbeau House
    B. Montfermeil
    C. Saint-Germain
    D. The Luxembourg Gardens

10. How does Valjean escape from the *Orion*?

    A. He bribes Javert
    B. He pretends to drown
    C. He scales a wall
    D. He steals a pair of silver candlesticks

REVIEW & RESOURCES

11. Why was Valjean originally arrested?

    A. He stole a loaf of bread
    B. He impersonated a manufacturer
    C. He kidnapped Cosette
    D. He abandoned Fantine

12. Why does Fantine lose her factory job?

    A. She tries to organize a union
    B. She is a prostitute
    C. She has an illegitimate daughter
    D. She spits in Madeleine's face

13. Why do the Thénardiers throw Gavroche out of their house?

    A. He steals from Montparnasse
    B. He is a supporter of Napoléon
    C. He is just another mouth to feed
    D. He is better dressed than Eponine and Azelma

14. How do Valjean and Marius escape from the barricade?

    A. Valjean carries Marius over a wall
    B. Valjean carries Marius through the sewers
    C. They flag down a passing carriage
    D. They pose as soldiers

15. Who is the leader of the Friends of the ABC?

    A. Enjolras
    B. Courfeyrac
    C. Tholomyès
    D. Fauchelevent

16. When are Marius and Gillenormand finally reconciled?

    A. After Marius marries Cosette
    B. After Marius agrees to change his political views
    C. After Marius recovers from his injuries
    D. Just before Marius finishes law school

17. Why does Marius feel indebted to Thénardier?

    A.   Thénardier's daughter Eponine saved Marius's life

    B.   He thinks that Thénardier saved his father's life

    C.   Thénardier gave him food when he was poor

    D.   Thénardier let him out of the sewer

18. Why does Gillenormand refuse to let Marius see his father?

    A.   Gillenormand and Pontmercy have different political views

    B.   Gillenormand does not want Marius to marry Cosette

    C.   Gillenormand knows that Pontmercy fathered Marius out of wedlock

    D.   Gillenormand thinks that Mabeuf would be a better father

19. Which of the following qualities does not describe the Thénardiers?

    A.   Poor

    B.   Desperate

    C.   Pious

    D.   Conniving

20. Why does Eponine give Cosette's address to Marius?

    A.   She wants money

    B.   She is in love with Marius

    C.   She is acting on a dare from Azelma

    D.   She wants Marius to deliver a letter to Cosette

21. Which of the following does not contribute to Valjean's decision to go to England?

    A.   Paris is growing increasingly politically unstable

    B.   Valjean is worried that he will lose Cosette

    C.   Valjean thinks that Thénardier is planning to rob him

    D.   Valjean believes that Marius will take part in the insurrection

REVIEW & RESOURCES

22. When Enjolras orders Javert's execution, what does Valjean do?

    A. He lets Javert go free
    B. He shoots Javert
    C. He throws Javert into the Seine
    D. He robs Javert

23. Where does Marius's father die?

    A. At the Battle of Waterloo
    B. On the barricade
    C. At his home
    D. In Madeleine's factory

24. When Javert tries to arrest Madeleine, what does Fantine do?

    A. She tries to fight Javert
    B. She leaves Montreuil-sur-mer
    C. She dies from shock
    D. She marries Marius

25. Which character does Hugo depict as an almost saintly figure?

    A. Jean Valjean
    B. Mme. Thénardier
    C. Javert
    D. Marius

ANSWER KEY:
1: B; 2: A; 3: C; 4: A; 5: B; 6: A; 7: C; 8: A; 9: D; 10: B; 11:
A; 12: C; 13: C; 14: B; 15: A; 16: C; 17: B; 18: A; 19: C; 20:
B; 21: D; 22: A; 23: C; 24: C; 25: A

SUGGESTIONS FOR FURTHER READING

BLOOM, HAROLD, ed. *Victor Hugo.* New York: Chelsea House Publishers, 1988.

BROMBERT, VICTOR H. *Victor Hugo and the Visionary Novel.* Cambridge, Massachusetts: Harvard University Press, 1984.

COLLINGHAM, H. A. C. *The July Monarchy: A Political History of France, 1830–1848.* New York: Longman, 1988.

GROSSMAN, KATHRYN M. LES MISÉRABLES: *Conversion, Revolution, Redemption.* New York: Twayne Publishers, 1996.

GROSSMAN, KATHRYN M. *Figuring Transcendence in* LES MISÉRABLES: *Hugo's Romantic Sublime.* Carbondale, Illinois: Southern Illinois University Press, 1994.

HAINE, W. SCOTT. *The History of France.* Westport, Connecticut: Greenwood Press, 2000.

PORTER, LAURENCE M. *Victor Hugo.* New York: Twayne Publishers, 1999.

ROBB, GRAHAM. *Victor Hugo.* New York: W. W. Norton, 1998.

REVIEW & RESOURCES

SparkNotes™ Literature Guides

1984
The Adventures of
    Huckleberry Finn
The Adventures of Tom
    Sawyer
The Aeneid
All Quiet on the
    Western Front
And Then There Were
    None
Angela's Ashes
Animal Farm
Anna Karenina
Anne of Green Gables
Anthem
Antony and Cleopatra
Aristotle's Ethics
As I Lay Dying
As You Like It
Atlas Shrugged
The Awakening
The Autobiography of
    Malcolm X
The Bean Trees
The Bell Jar
Beloved
Beowulf
Billy Budd
Black Boy
Bless Me, Ultima
The Bluest Eye
Brave New World
The Brothers
    Karamazov
The Call of the Wild
Candide
The Canterbury Tales
Catch-22
The Catcher in the Rye
The Chocolate War
The Chosen
Cold Mountain
Cold Sassy Tree
The Color Purple
The Count of Monte
    Cristo
Crime and Punishment
The Crucible
Cry, the Beloved
    Country
Cyrano de Bergerac
David Copperfield

Death of a Salesman
The Death of Socrates
The Diary of a Young
    Girl
A Doll's House
Don Quixote
Dr. Faustus
Dr. Jekyll and Mr. Hyde
Dracula
Dune
East of Eden
Edith Hamilton's
    Mythology
Emma
Ethan Frome
Fahrenheit 451
Fallen Angels
A Farewell to Arms
Farewell to Manzanar
Flowers for Algernon
For Whom the Bell
    Tolls
The Fountainhead
Frankenstein
The Giver
The Glass Menagerie
Gone With the Wind
The Good Earth
The Grapes of Wrath
Great Expectations
The Great Gatsby
Greek Classics
Grendel
Gulliver's Travels
Hamlet
The Handmaid's Tale
Hard Times
Harry Potter and the
    Sorcerer's Stone
Heart of Darkness
Henry IV, Part I
Henry V
Hiroshima
The Hobbit
The House of Seven
    Gables
I Know Why the Caged
    Bird Sings
The Iliad
Inferno
Inherit the Wind
Invisible Man

Jane Eyre
Johnny Tremain
The Joy Luck Club
Julius Caesar
The Jungle
The Killer Angels
King Lear
The Last of the
    Mohicans
Les Miserables
A Lesson Before Dying
The Little Prince
Little Women
Lord of the Flies
The Lord of the Rings
Macbeth
Madame Bovary
A Man for All Seasons
The Mayor of
    Casterbridge
The Merchant of Venice
A Midsummer Night's
    Dream
Moby Dick
Much Ado About
    Nothing
My Antonia
Narrative of the Life of
    Frederick Douglass
Native Son
The New Testament
Night
Notes from
    Underground
The Odyssey
The Oedipus Plays
Of Mice and Men
The Old Man and the
    Sea
The Old Testament
Oliver Twist
The Once and Future
    King
One Day in the Life of
    Ivan Denisovich
One Flew Over the
    Cuckoo's Nest
One Hundred Years of
    Solitude
Othello
Our Town
The Outsiders

Paradise Lost
A Passage to India
The Pearl
The Picture of Dorian
    Gray
Poe's Short Stories
A Portrait of the Artist
    as a Young Man
Pride and Prejudice
The Prince
A Raisin in the Sun
The Red Badge of
    Courage
The Republic
Richard III
Robinson Crusoe
Romeo and Juliet
The Scarlet Letter
A Separate Peace
Silas Marner
Sir Gawain and the
    Green Knight
Slaughterhouse-Five
Snow Falling on Cedars
Song of Solomon
The Sound and the Fury
Steppenwolf
The Stranger
Streetcar Named
    Desire
The Sun Also Rises
A Tale of Two Cities
The Taming of the
    Shrew
The Tempest
Tess of the d'Ubervilles
Their Eyes Were
    Watching God
Things Fall Apart
The Things They
    Carried
To Kill a Mockingbird
To the Lighthouse
Treasure Island
Twelfth Night
Ulysses
Uncle Tom's Cabin
Walden
War and Peace
Wuthering Heights
A Yellow Raft in Blue
    Water